Going Indie

A Complete Guide to Becoming an
Independent Software Developer

Brian Schrader

SkyRocket Software, LLC

Going Indie

by Brian Schrader

Printed in the United States of America

Published by SkyRocket Software, LLC

This book may be purchased for educational, business, or sales promotional use. Online editions are also available where books are sold.

Editor: Jennifer M. Sardina, MS LCGC

Cover Designer: Owais Uz Zaman

Proofreaders: Nathaniel Arellano, Marco Martinez, Moline Schrader

Special thanks to: Dave Mote

November 2020:   First Edition

To my sister Bailey for her love and her smile, my father Kevin for his focus and his nerdy passion, and my mother Moline for her drive and her eternal support.

This book is for you.

TABLE OF CONTENTS

Developing Your Ideas

Technical Considerations

EXITING THE CAVE

Let's Design a Thing

Architecture by Example

Preface

To be independent is to carve one's own path, to forge one's own destiny. Independent software developers are those who release software under their own name, often through their own companies, and they may even turn a profit doing so. Occasionally independent developers are incredibly lucky and are able to make their entire living by writing their own software, while the majority release independent software as a hobby or as a side-business while working a typical job. Others release software as only part of an independent persona; these developers are often found writing books, recording podcasts, and giving talks in addition to shipping software. Those of you who decide to journey into the relatively untamed wilds of the independent world can either choose to follow trails carved by others or strike out on your own. How far you venture into these woods is for you to decide. Go as far as your intuition dares and your capacity allows. To create software and release it to the world under your own banner is perhaps one of the greatest freedoms our chosen profession offers us. Like writers, poets, and musicians, the work that developers are capable of is akin to magic. We create something from nothing, we build and shape the world around us, and we can solve problems for ourselves and share those solutions with others for little additional expense.

Be warned, these wilds can be treacherous. Many who venture forth come back empty handed, and some do not come back at all. This book will not show you how to cross the wilds. It does not provide you a map, for no such maps exist. Instead, this book aims to be both a guide to show you the most dangerous places, and a set of tools you can use along your journey. The advice and guidance given here was won through personal experience, careful surveying, and self reflection. It is useful, but it should not be considered absolute. Mine is but one of many paths through the woods, a journey I am still on. You will not walk the same road, and so should not seek to emulate my every footstep. This book is also not a map listing the locations of every steep cliff or venomous snake in the land (hopefully you will avoid the hazards I've faced, but you will surely encounter your own). It's a guide that teaches you instead how to read the winds, follow the game trails, and find fresh water. On this journey, stumbling is assured. You will encounter hardship. The only question is whether you will learn from your mistakes and keep going. Those of you who persevere, who take the trek and emerge on the other side, will discover just how rewarding becoming an independent software developer can actually be.

WHO THIS BOOK IS FOR

While there are a great many people who would probably find this book of some use, it is primarily targeted at software developers with an express desire to break out of their current grind and start a business either by themselves or with a small group of friends. Now, there are lots of various kinds of businesses, and not all are within the scope of this book. Here we will focus on small software businesses, which (although less often discussed) are the more practical option for a single individual or limited team. We'll cover business models, pricing tiers, technological tradeoffs, and personal motivation. To provide some real-life context, we'll dive into the technical details of building, hosting, and maintaining a software service using Nine9s, a service I built and launched in 2020, as an example.

WHO THIS BOOK IS NOT FOR

Readers looking for the best ways to apply for Venture Capital, how to manage hockey-stick growth, or those seeking insight into the process and nuances of corporate IPOs are going to be rather disappointed by this book. We don't discuss data mining or user data extraction, nor will we talk about how to increase "engagement" or optimize our data harvesting model. We will instead discuss the fine art of providing goods or services to a market willing to pay real money to access and use them. As such, this confines the scope of our business to those that are more traditional, slow-growing, and that are profitable on their own merit. If you're looking for the Silicon Valley dream, I suggest you look elsewhere.

WHAT YOU'LL LEARN

This book covers topics ranging from marketing to software development from motivation to system administration. You'll learn the differences between certain types of businesses, how to think about and design products, how to structure pricing tiers, how to design maintainable data models, how to host your software and run servers, and how to market your product before, during, and after launch. The goal of this book is to provide readers with a complete understanding of the tools and experience needed to take a product from idea to launch and beyond while assuming some level of software development experience. Running a software business requires surprisingly little knowledge of software and software development. There's a lot more involved in creating a successful business than simply building a good app or service. Here we will fill in those gaps with knowledge gained from years of experience, develop your intuition around your business, and design user-centric features that benefit both you and your users.

While we will be discussing some technical aspects in this book, it is assumed that the reader already has some proficiency or experience in software development (although no specific expertise is required). This is not a programming guide or computer science textbook, but we'll cover a few useful tips and tricks that can help you build your software more effectively.

LICENSE

The content of this book is licensed under a Creative Commons Attribution 4.0 International License.

This means that you're free to repurpose and reuse the contents of this book for commercial and non-commercial purposes. Your attributions drive the spread of this knowledge. Attributions help sell copies of this book which, in turn, help me to continue giving back to the communities that have given so much to me.

HOW TO MAKE AN ATTRIBUTION

According to the terms of the license used by this book:

The following attribution would be sensible:

> *Going Indie* by Brian Schrader.
>
> Copyright Brian Schrader 2020, 978-1-63625-958-1

CONVENTIONS USED IN THIS BOOK

Sections denoted in a dotted border are considered callouts. These sections are loosely tied to the surrounding content and mostly exist to provide additional context or warn readers of possible complications that may arise from the instructions provided. Callouts may also seek to address anticipated concerns or feedback, if necessary.

> This is an example callout seeking to provide additional context.

Sections indented and denoted with a darker background are block-quotes, a large section of text pulled from another source. These quotes may serve to provide advice or they may be referred to by the text surrounding it.

> This is an example of a block-quote.

HOW TO CONTACT ME

Feel free to contact me using the email address listed on my blog: brianschrader.com. I'd be happy to answer any questions or provide feedback. If you have questions or comments about the contents of this book, or if you'd like to share your story or your work with me, please feel free to get in touch. It's always a joy to hear from readers.

Like it says on my site, I can be slow to check my email and therefore can't always guarantee a prompt response. I welcome any suggestions, feedback, and critique so long as it is constructive and relevant.

Please send all hate-mail to `/dev/null`.

You &

Your Product &

Your Company

Going Indie

The Dream

If you're reading this, then you probably want to learn how to become a successful independent developer. You already know how to build software. Now, you're looking for the secrets, tips, tricks, and advice that can promote you from simple developer to a higher echelon, an exclusive club where you can release your software successfully and independently, free of corporate over-lords and dishonest industry practices. You may see indie devs on Twitter talking about their software, you might read their blogs and you want in on their game, or you might just have a great idea and the ability to build it, but you're lacking the insight, the knowledge, or the courage to take that next step to publish and release your software independently. I've been developing, publishing, and releasing software independently for years, and I've been in both of those categories at various times. I've learned a lot about the software industry. I've discovered a number of strategies that help me build better software and help me run my business. That said, I've also discovered a greater number of tips and tricks that definitely do not work. I've found a number of ways to waste time and money chasing goals that aren't helpful, and crucially, I've uncovered methods that help me recover from those bad decisions. This is what I offer you in this book: not a guarantee of success, not a perfect guide, but a trove of methodologies, strategies, and life experiences gained by doing nearly everything wrong the first time. Importantly, I also do not offer you an endpoint. I'm still on my own journey to independence and success; I'm just further down the road looking back at the path I've charted and offering you a chance to avoid the same pitfalls I unknowingly stumbled into. In this way, this book is less like a memoir of my journey; it's not a look back on the road to some glamorous end. It is more like a journal written while the tale is still being told, an account written during the struggle untainted by the rose-colored glasses of nostalgia, instead seen with the clear eyes of one still trapped in the fog along a path to an unknown destination. Like you, I am on a quest. Perhaps, by the end of this, both of us will be closer to our goal.

INDEPENDENCE AND SUCCESS

Independence means different things to different people, as does the term Independent Developer. To some, independent development might refer to small companies with a few employees passionately making software for a dedicated audience. Companies like Rogue Amoeba and The Omni Group fit this description. They employ potentially tens of people to build powerful and unique software for a large audience. To others, independent development might instead refer to individuals like Manton Reece, Maciej Cegłowski, Marco Arment, and others that make a living by selling software under their own name and through their own companies. Finally, independent developers might simply refer to anyone who makes and releases software to the world under their own name regardless of whether that software supports them financially. In these cases, independent developers may earn some form of income from their software, perhaps even significant supplemental income, while others may choose to release their software for free. In the same way that in order to earn the title of open source contributor one need only correct a typo in an open source project's documentation, an independent developer need only to release software under their own name to be considered truly independent.

As with any nuanced discussion of a complex topic, before the conversation can begin, terms need to be defined. For our purposes, we'll constrain our definition of Independent Developer to mean an individual who releases software under their own name to make a profit. This is a pretty conventional definition, but it's important to remember that it isn't the only definition. We're intentionally excluding those who build software for free and those who employ other developers as part of their endeavor. This limited definition will allow us to better explore and better understand the benefits, the considerations, and the constraints that real independent developers face. After all, if we were to employ a broader definition it would be difficult to meaningfully generalize about the challenges and opportunities that such a group of developers would face, and it would be even harder to proffer advice.

At times, this book will include brief discussions that broaden our definition of Independent Developer to include small teams of around three to four people. This is because, while most of the advice and guidance in this book does generalize out to groups, in some cases there may be nuances that are worth clarifying. Lots of independent developers work with friends or others in the community towards a shared goal, and while this book is primarily targeted at those working alone, the sheer popularity of group projects and my own experience with them means that when there are significant exceptions and additions it would be negligent to omit them.

Success, like independence, also changes based on how you define it. What you mean when you use the word "successful" will have a significant impact on the decisions you choose to make during your time as an independent developer. If your image of success is to become the next Yelp, Lyft, or Apple, then this book is not for you. There are countless other writers who teach the fine art of founding Silicon Valley Start-Ups, applying for venture capital, choosing co-founders, building your team, pivoting your service, going public, and getting bought out by Google. This is not that. Here we will focus on more mundane, but also much more attainable, goals.

OUR APPROACH

Throughout this book, we'll take a look at what it takes to start and to run an independent software company, one with zero employees and no venture capital or angel funding. A company that makes software for people who pay money to use it. Such a paradigm may be relatively unheard of in the Valley, but still very much exists. There are countless examples of developers who build and sell products and services on the Web through their own companies. Some developers make screencasts or podcasts, others build apps or services, some are bloggers or published authors, and still more do a combination. These people are often working by themselves, or with their family or friends to make their living on the Web. Some have small teams, some don't. Quite a few have persisted through the ages, first emerging from the primeval ooze of the Web in the 90s, others are as old as the App Store, while plenty more have just begun. These companies typically have one thing in common — no matter what they do or sell, they are founded and run by people who build simple, bespoke, artisanal software.

They started with an idea, they worked hard, they got a little lucky, they got knocked down, and they kept trying.

While there are a lot of ways to build a business on the Web, in this book we'll look at just one: Software as a Service. We'll discuss how services differ from traditional products. We'll look at how to develop an idea for a software service and how to take that idea through to launch and beyond. As a developer, you may believe that building the software is the most important part, but you'd be wrong. Ultimately, your software is a small part of your business. How you choose to design and implement your software is important, but so is the payment structure, software infrastructure, UI design, branding, marketing plan, business plan, and feature roadmap. There are lots of aspects to running a business, and you'll need to do them all, at least for now. We'll look at how to balance each of these roles, how to judge your decisions, and how to think about your business holistically. We'll cover some tips and tricks to help you balance your day-job while starting your business and how to extract the most out of your limited time by building a routine and tracking your progress. We'll cover launching your software, promoting it, marketing it, how to build an audience, and how to deliver quality software on a budget and on a limited schedule.

Advice and explanations can get dull when served alone. While it packs a lot of nutrients, simple advice oatmeal is pretty bland. That's why, throughout this book, we're going to sprinkle on some real examples and statistics from my own software business experience and the experiences of other developers in the software community. We'll look at examples from a variety of projects built by myself and others, discuss the benefits and tradeoffs of these different approaches, contrast these real-world examples with the myths surrounding indie development, and we'll use these examples to inform our decision making and set our expectations accordingly.

Even the most successful indie developers out there didn't start out that way. Most built up their business while working another job, doing consulting work, or some mixture of both. The truly lucky made it big in another endeavor or otherwise had the resources to quit their job at the beginning and build their business from scratch. Personally, I have no experience making it big and building a business from scratch with the proceeds, so I can't speak to the challenges inherent in that approach. I have worked a full-time job while building the majority of my business, and I've taken a few short extended breaks to redouble my efforts when the opportunity arose. We'll be focusing here on the most common scenario and one I have years of experience with: moonlighting; working nights and weekends, after work, to build your business and launch your software.

If it sounds like running a business is going to be a lot of work, that's because it is. However, there are lots of things you can do to simplify and to make things easier. There are lots of shortcuts you can take, and lots of problems you can kick down the road. You just have to know where to look (and where to kick). Staying motivated is important, so important that a significant portion of this book deals with understanding motivation and cultivating it. Running a business is hard, and you have only yourself and your own internal motivations to keep you going. Once you know how to stay motivated, we'll discuss the most common problems you'll encounter, how to avoid them if you can, and how to push past them if you can't. Through it all, it's important to stay focused and not be too hard on yourself. There are going to be decisions that you have to make with little information, and you may regret those decisions later on. Always remember that your decisions appear clearer and better informed in hindsight, the choices easier to distinguish. The right decision always seems more obvious as time goes on, but you don't get to make decisions with any foreknowledge. You make them with the information you have at the time, and there's no point in beating yourself up later over questions you couldn't possibly be expected to answer. The process of starting a business is challenging and full of unknowns, some of which you might see coming and some that are going to completely blindside you. You're going to be asking yourself to tackle a number of new things, most of which you've probably never done before. Learning is going to be a constant; one of the very few in this process. You'll work hard, you'll struggle, and you'll get knocked down. That's ok. It happens to everyone. But if you succeed, whatever that word means to you, then it will have all been worth it.

WHAT IS SUCCESS?

Despite their intelligence and talent, many people with the goal of starting an indie business end up failing. Software, especially on the Web, is dominated by enormous companies with thousands of engineers and frankly, with one person (or a small team) you're just not going to be able to compete with them directly. You need to do what they can't. Large companies, even with dedicated product teams, often lack a certain attention to detail, especially on their smaller projects. Teams there are tasked with maintaining multiple small projects, or only work on them for a small portion of their time. At Apple and Google for example, teams are often told to develop an app or service and, after launch, only update it once a year. This is where you have the advantage.

Success on the Web doesn't actually need to be all that successful. Depending on how you price your service and how much it costs to run, you can become profitable with just a few hundred dedicated users; something that companies like Google, Apple, or even Atlasssian will never be able to do. A company's size is often an asset, but it can also be a hinderance. As the size of a company grows, so must the scope of its software. Large companies simply can't afford to chase smaller fish, but you can. This is your competitive advantage: they may have more resources and more bandwidth, but you have more focus. Finding a niche and filling it is critical. Don't worry if your software isn't all things to all people, instead think about how it could be one really great thing to a select group of people. The number of features you support, in most cases, just isn't all that relevant and can often make your product or service harder to market and sell. Focus on solving a small number of problems, and solving them well. Quality will win out in the end.

> It turns out that staying small offers some surprising advantages, not just in the day-to-day experience of work, but in marketing and getting customers to love your project. Best of all, there's plenty more room at the bottom.
>
> If your goal is to do meaningful work you love, you may be much closer to realizing your dreams than you think.
>
> Barely Succeed! It's Easier! - Maciej Cegłowski

Too often, even in well-funded Start-Ups, founders try to tackle a problem-set that is too broad or unfocused. Instead of doing one or two things well, they do twenty things poorly, leaving their customers underwhelmed. It's important to keep your ideas realistic and not be caught in the trap of dreaming about the future too far in advance. If you're planning to eventually expand and hire that's great! But don't spend the majority of your focus and energy planning out features you might eventually have the team build. You don't have that team now, and if you lose focus, you never will.

THE GOLDILOCKS ZONE

Is the product you want to launch within your capabilities? Can you actually build it? These aren't necessarily technical questions. Without upfront financial backing, the product you choose to build needs to be something that can be developed, launched, maintained, upgraded, promoted, marketed, and administered by you (or your small team). There's a lot that you can achieve with just yourself, a great idea, and some focused effort, but competing against multi-national corporations is not one of them.

Technical acumen aside, there's simply a lot of behind-the-scenes work involved in creating a successful product and company. Non-technical work will inevitably take up a chunk of your time and your motivation, so smaller projects focused on a narrow problem-set are usually best, especially if you're just starting out. Now, that's not to say that large projects can't be done. It instead puts an upper limit on the scale of your projects, and limits the size of the features you can deliver in a given time. Large scale projects are possible, but they will take longer. If you're aiming to tackle something big, be sure to break up the main features into smaller pieces. In order to do that though, you need to work diligently for months. To do that, you have to stay motivated.

Staying Motivated

Forming a company, developing a product, and launching software are all important parts of the process of becoming independent. But no matter how good your idea is, how popular your service becomes, or how much money you make from it, without motivation, everything else is meaningless. Motivation is what drives you to keep pushing forward, motivation is what gets you through the difficult times, and motivation is what ultimately builds your product. Without it, nothing else can happen.

Like currency, your motivation is a finite resource You earn it over time through positive feedback and achieving goals. You spend it by working long hours and struggling to finish burdensome and boring tasks. Without revenue, external pressures, or co-founders your only motivation is internal and, like starting funds, you can easily burn through all of your initial motivation too early. In this scenario, you can find yourself with nothing substantial, and without the will to keep going. But if you manage your motivational budget carefully you can overcome even the toughest challenges. Managing and rekindling motivation is a constant process that never really stops. Most developers, and in fact most people in general, don't give much thought to their own internal motivations: what they mean, how they're fed, or how to focus them. This is the primary reason why so many projects fail. In the Open Source world, it's not uncommon to see popular projects abandoned because the creator has lost the will to keep improving it, even if the money is flowing in. You-Tubers, Bloggers, Podcasters, Writers, and Developers face this same challenge. Often synonymous with burnout, the result is the same: the project ends.

These next sections will focus exclusively on motivation: how to think about it, how to manage it, and what to do when it runs out. This advice comes largely from personal experience. I've found myself about to run out of motivation time and time again. On occasion, I've run out completely and projects have died because of it. Other times I've been able to claw my way back out of the deep hole and move things forward. Hopefully, with the right foreknowledge, you can avoid the traps that ensnared me and develop tools to help you get out of similar traps. Starting a business and building a product, like so many other things is a journey across unknown seas. Some find their way across by dumb luck, others with sheer determination or through careful planning and experience. This discussion should give you the tools you need to navigate the treacherous waters ahead. A sturdy, well-built ship and detailed maps are crucial in determining whether your expedition will succeed, but the whole endeavor is for naught if the winds of motivation don't fill your sails.

THE RIGHT MINDSET

I didn't think much about my own mindset before starting a business. In fact, it took years of trial and error before I discovered how important my mindset is to my software, my company, and my well-being. Before building anything, especially something that takes months or possibly years to complete, it's critical to develop your mindset, or at least to become aware of how the decisions you're making effect you and your internal motivation.

You and your attitude are more influential in determining whether your product will launch than most other factors. Technology can be changed, software can be rewritten, hosting platforms can be swapped, companies can be bought and sold, if you have the will and motivation to do it. Motivation isn't something that can just be turned on and off either. It's a scarce and valuable resource that must be extracted, refined, and forged into useful energy, and like natural resources it can run out. This is the ultimate existential threat for anyone running a business whether with co-founders or alone. Your motivation, dedication, and drive to work on or complete a project is finite. It can be cultivated and grown, but it can also be abused.

Instead of the tortured metaphor of mineral extraction, it's useful to think of your motivation as a forest. Your mental state and well-being can't be compartmentalized and isolated from itself. Everything in your life influences everything else to some extent. The trees within the forest supply all of the motivation you have for all aspects of your life, not just the motivation for your side projects. On its own the forest grows slowly, seeds spread and new trees grow, occasional fires sweep through and decimate the forest, but with time it will regrow. Through deliberate effort you can plant new trees and maintain the undergrowth. You can use the wood from these trees to build your business, but cut down too many and you're risking disaster in other personal endeavors. Use too little and you may never finish your projects; the undergrowth can then become overgrown and untamed laying the perfect ground for a spark to ignite a wildfire, destroying everything you've built. Manage your forest carefully. Plant new trees and watch for smoke in the distance. Once your motivation is gone (the trees cut down or burned to ash) you're left with nothing. There's no quick remedy. Only through the slow march of time will the forest regrow.

SETTING GOALS

Setting goals may seem like a trope of business project planning, but that's for good reason. The wrong goals can doom a project, while setting the right goals can prepare you to overcome steep odds and obstacles. Business people have lots of words and acronyms to describe good goal creating processes, and to define what a "good goal" even is. Ignore all that. When you're trying to improve or preserve your motivation, let these three ideals be your guide. Goals should be simple, specific, and timely.

Simple goals may sound almost mundane, but crafting such goals is much harder (and more beneficial to your success) than it sounds. Let's take a look at a few examples of simple but specific goals you may need to set for yourself:

- Configure Nginx to redirect HTTP to HTTPS
- Sketch User Profile page
- Reply to yesterday's customer service email

It's important to set goals that go beyond just the technical aspects. It's also important that these goals are straightforward. You know what needs to be done, and you know what it means to complete the task. That said, simple doesn't mean easy-to-complete, just easy-to-understand. A key reason for breaking up large or complex tasks into simple ones is to help your teammates understand what the task entails regardless of whether your team is a few co-founders, or just past, present, and future you. Notice how specific the goals laid out in the above section are. The goal isn't Set up Nginx, instead it's Configure Nginx to redirect HTTP to HTTPS. It's a goal that can be completed. Who on earth knows when Nginx will ever be properly set up? It could be years before you stop tweaking settings for new features. Instead, the goal lays out a specific feature we want: Redirect HTTP traffic to HTTPS. Notice that there are no details on how to redirect it, that's a bridge we can cross when it's time to actually do the task. When laying out goals; is there a clear way to determine that the task has been completed? How would you test it? In this case, we want to make a plain-text HTTP request to the server and have the server respond with a "301 Moved" response that redirects a visitor to instead use HTTPS. Done! Specific goals make it easier to understand when a task is complete and can be taken off the to-do list. If you find that you've finished nearly every aspect of a task, but you can't mark it as complete yet because of co-dependent tasks or an outside delay, try breaking it into two parts. Mark one as complete and leave the other one on the pile. The longer you let big tasks sit in your to-do list, the more overwhelming that list becomes. The length of your to-do list is more psychologically damaging than the items on it. A long list is exhausting to look at even if every one of the items is two-thirds complete. Simple, specific, and timely goals ensure that your to-do list is in constant flux. Items are always coming on the list, but more importantly, they are also getting taken off or marked as complete.

Small goals that can be accomplished quickly are a godsend for recouping motivation. Completing timely goals, whether they be shippable features, internal optimizations, or even simple coding tricks can generate a feeling of accomplishment and forward momentum The Nginx task from before is a good example. If your site was being served over plain-text HTTP (though I'd hope it wasn't) simply moving to HTTPS is a straightforward, simple, and achievable goal that can often be accomplished in a couple hours. Sprinkling a few of these goals into your timelines can be a lifeline while drowning in the abyss of a big new feature or massive refactor. Be careful though, too many small features can also be a distraction from the real work you need to do and the small dopamine hits they provide could quickly become addictive. This becomes especially apparent if you focus on internal tasks like code refactors or tooling improvements. We'll cover more of this later on, but for now be warned: too many developers get lost building tools for themselves and never ship a product for their users. While it's true in certain cases that a few hours of scripting can save you days of work, it's also true that you can spend days of clever scripting and only save yourself seconds of menial work. Your job is not to make your own life as easy as possible, if that was true then this book would be mainly irrelevant; your actual job is to ship quality software for your users.

Setting the right goals can be the key to pulling yourself or your team out of a rut. During the development of Adventurer's Codex, which at the time was worked on by a small team consisting of myself and two friends, we were in the middle of a particularly painful refactor, when it became apparent to all of us that our motivation was rapidly declining. The task we'd decided to tackle was far larger than we'd anticipated and involved a lot more refactoring than we'd hoped. It was tough to keep going. We worked primarily on the weekends and it had been months since we'd shipped a user-facing feature. We considered taking a hiatus or just giving up entirely. Without motivation, everything else was pointless. So we changed course. We pivoted. For the next week we focused instead on shipping a small feature to our users. We chose something that would be straightforward to develop, easy to merge back into the refactor we were working on, and something that we'd wanted for a while. That small feature gave us the chance to push a release, announce the new feature, get excited about the feedback, and keep on plowing through the larger refactor with a bit more energy than before. No matter what stage your project is in (especially if you're not yet getting paid for your work), motivation and positive feedback loops are the compensation you are awarded for a job well done. Getting paid in actual currency is obviously the goal, but when that's still over the horizon, motivation is all you really have. Setting good goals is perhaps one of the easiest ways to renew your motivation and put the wind back in your sails.

TRACKING YOUR PROGRESS

It's easy to be lax with project management when it's only you. Often times you'll have an intuitive sense of what needs to be done, and that believe other things will get handled naturally as they come up. Fight the urge to keep everything in your head. It may seem like overkill to keep detailed task lists, extensive project plans, feature tickets, accounting spreadsheets, or deployment checklists. It isn't. There are a number of great tools out there to help you organize and track your business, just be careful not to introduce tools that don't serve a purpose. Sometimes a pad of paper works best. Jot down, in whatever app or notebook you prefer, any new features, bugs, gotchas, future implementation details, pricing changes, logo designs, etc. Use whatever method works best, just document it somewhere. Depending on the idea, I keep notes in a notebook, in the iOS Notes app, or on my office mirror in dry-erase marker. How you keep your own notes is up to you, just don't keep them in your head. The reasons for this are somewhat obvious. Writing things down frees up your brain-space to work on other tasks, while ensuring that those things aren't simply forgotten. When your ideas relate to newly identified bugs, implementation ideas, or other nuanced changes, taking notes increases communication between past, present, and future you. It's not uncommon for developers to solve a problem in their heads, complete with a few important nuances or gotchas, but later when they go to actually write the code, they've forgotten some key aspect. In most scenarios this results in the feature to taking even longer to build, as you must now rediscover your past cleverness. Speaking from experience, you'll also be more likely to miss key details of the feature or bug, and worsen the situation by just blindly coding.

PICKING YOURSELF UP

Much of the proceeding sections have focused on how to stay motivated during the long process of building your project, but staying on the horse is only one part of the journey. What happens when you fall off? Losing your motivation, burning out, and wanting to give up are common scenarios for many people during large projects, especially life-changing ones like starting a business or building a commercial product. If you find yourself in any of these scenarios, you're not alone. From my personal experience, it seems like every time I've committed myself to a project I've gone through a similar motivational rollercoaster. Eventually there comes a time when the initial drive is gone. For me, it always seems to come a few weeks after launch. The excitement of building and launching a new thing, the rush of getting that first feedback, the push to resolve any launch-day bugs and get out a few new features; all of that is gone. The project begins to slide into the long, slow maintenance and improvement phase. If your launch went well, this transition can take months or even years to begin, but if it went poorly (something we'll cover in later chapters) then it can set in almost immediately.

A bad launch or a long dry spell without new users signing up are challenging experiences to endure. Long, difficult refactors or upgrades are similarly draining. During these times you may feel the urge to give up and move on. And sometimes that's best. It's not inspiring to hear, but it is possible to paint yourself into a corner and it may not be worth it to continue. Most times though, it's better to first take a step back from the problem, reevaluate your progress and your goals, and try something new or different. One reason I advise so strongly against refactoring large segments of your code is precisely because of the motivational hit that may result from having to fix and rework long-standing parts of your application for little to no customer benefit. It doesn't feel great to spend months on something no one will see, especially if you're already weighed down by something like a bad launch.

If you find yourself stuck in the midst of a large refactor or big feature that you just can't seem to finish, ask yourself the following questions: What is the goal of what I'm doing? Does this need to be done now? Changing tack in the middle of a huge feature isn't ideal. A lot of times it's easier to just finish what you were working on instead of starting something new, but other times, even if you're right near the end of a feature, you just can't finish it. This could be because of a technical limitation, a huge learning curve, or just simple apathy. In those cases it's best to shelve what you're doing, take a break and when you come back, work on something that can boost your motivation. It can be something silly like a few color changes, redesigning an old page, adding a new help article, or writing a simple feature you've wanted for a while. Choose an activity that seems likely to give you a taste of the satisfaction you've been lacking.

REACHING OUT

Building an entire company from the ground up can get lonely at times. There's no one to help you solve important problems, no one to bounce ideas off of, and no one to excite you about the future except yourself. Some of this is par for the course, at least until you start getting users and feedback, but some of it isn't. There are lots of other developers, entrepreneurs, and small business owners out there and while they often can't help you with technical issues, they can offer advice, support, feedback, and maybe even publicity for your company.

In no way should this section be construed to imply that you should spam lots of indie-devs with shameless requests for publicity. Instead, spend time getting involved in the community you're trying to enter. Building relationships with similar companies and like-minded people will not only give you valuable insight into the ins-and-outs of the market you're trying to enter, but the sense of camaraderie can also help you maintain motivation and retain a positive outlook. If you're looking to get feedback from people you know or follow, send them a promo-code and let them try out your service, or start a beta program and allow people to solicit feedback. Reaching out for help like this isn't shameless at all, companies large and small do it all the time. There are tons of people out there who love trying out new tech and giving feedback. Leverage those communities to build goodwill, improve your product, and garner initial interest.

Working alone doesn't have to be lonely. Over time you may gain new tools to address common problems. You'll also become a better member of the community at large. So much of your business' success lies not on how good your product is, but in who uses it and who talks about it. Once you do establish yourself, others may reach out to you in turn and when they do, remember to pay it forward. You'll be helping yourself and a whole new generation of developers and entrepreneurs.

THIS SOUNDS LIKE WORK

Treating a passion project like work may take some of the fun away, but it's crucial for the long term success of the project. Task lists and schedules impose a structure, a method to the madness that is creation. One of the easiest ways to stay motivated and productive, whether you're working full-time on your business or just nights and weekends, is to impose a schedule on yourself. Schedules enforce a structure and keep you focused. If you're working on a feature or design when you could be watching TV, doing chores, or hanging out with friends, then you'll be consistently distracted by those other things. Set aside time to work. It can be as little as two hours once a week, or as much as eight hours a day. Add that time to your calendar and tell yourself and others that you're working during that time. Not only will they be less likely to interrupt you, but telling others helps reenforce the idea in your own mind that the time is designated for work. Try to make your schedule consistent. Instead of scheduling two hours at some point during the week, set aside a specific evening when things are less likely to get in the way. Consistency breeds consistency. Keep to that schedule as long and as often as you can, but realize it's ok to fail occasionally. Life is messy, especially if you're moonlighting. If life changes, your schedule should change with it. It's important to find the balance between being consistent and adaptable when necessary. Learning to stay on the horse is not the only part of the process that matters. You're going to fall off, a lot. It's just as important to learn how to fall, how to brush yourself off, and how to get back on.

Another part of enforcing a consistent work-habit is having a dedicated workspace. A good office has these things:

- An isolated, quiet space that is used for work

- A door you can close

- A dedicated desk, and monitor (ergonomic for you)

- A window for some natural light

- Good air circulation (fan, window, etc)

- A good work chair

- Storage for papers, legal documents, forms, etc

Most people, myself included, don't have access to all of this in their homes, and that's ok. Try to check as many of those boxes as possible. Carve out any dedicated space in your home (or try working from another location). Separating your work and home life is crucial. If your video games are nearby, it's harder to resist the urge to play them. That's not to say that your workspace should be completely spartan. I play guitar, and I like to have one close by to play when I'm feeling tired and need a break. Regardless, your workspace needs to feel like a workspace. It should convey the impression that a professional works there, because you are a professional, even if you're only working on the project in your spare time.

Isolating work from leisure is key. A separate desk in a shared space is a good first step. The goal is to trick your brain. To let yourself know that when you're sitting at this specific desk, you are working on your project. Avoid surfing the Web or playing games in this space. If you need to, get up and move to the couch to do that. It sounds simple, but creating a dedicated workspace can really help improve your focus and motivation. There's a reason that offices exist. They impose a work schedule and they lack other leisurely activities for a reason: to help people stay focused. Modern companies have spent millions of dollars studying worker productivity, and you can use their tricks for yourself. Even if, like me, you dislike offices and office culture there are great insights you can gain from how they are structured. Find what works best for you. Jot ideas down on sticky-notes, schedule team meetings with yourself, or just set aside a dedicated office space. The goal is to make yourself more productive; the optimal way to achieve that productivity will depend on you.

Starting Your Business

Doing business on the Internet can be challenging. This is particularly true due to the fact that the Internet and the Web are governed by lots of different regulatory and legislative authorities. Starting a business is complex and difficult enough; starting a Web-based business is even more so. There are a number of important things you'll need to do in order to start and run a legitimate business on the Web. Some of these aspects will be financial, others legal, and some organizational. In this section, we'll cover a few best practices for starting and managing your business, and dive into the options you have if you decide to form a company. This will include details around the legal and organizational tradeoffs between each approach. In doing this, I aim to dispel some of the myths around starting a business and help you overcome any uncertainty.

Most people, and I would wager most developers, find the legal aspects of starting a business to be among the most intimidating and off-putting. While there is good reason to be cautious about what kind of business you want to form and how you run it, the process itself isn't all that complicated. Once you know the basics —what kinds of businesses you can choose from, the benefits and drawbacks of each, and what's required of you— the actual work is pretty simple and straightforward, although still painstakingly slow at times. If you feel concerned or put off by the idea now, hopefully I can convince you that starting a business is nothing to be afraid of. Over the years, I've been involved in a few different kinds of Web based businesses and I've seen much of the good, the bad, and the ugly that each type brings along with it. I've done business as a sole-proprietor, under two different kinds of Limited Liability Company (LLC) in two different U.S. states, and I've held ownership in a standard C-Corp. If that all means nothing to you, that's fine. We'll discuss each of these options in turn and what they mean for you.

The advice here isn't a substitute for your own research. I live in the United States, so all of my experience comes from starting businesses there. In the U.S. laws and regulations surrounding the responsibilities and legal liabilities of different types of businesses vary wildly state-to-state. The information I present here is from my own personal experience as a resident of California and may not be relevant to those living in other states, though the general layout is most likely similar. My goal here isn't to provide you with a fool-proof legal strategy. I'm not a legal expert and this is not legal advice. Instead, my goal is to demystify the process, explain the general types of business arrangements, and give you the tools you need to do the research and make your own judgements.

TERMINOLOGY

Before we can dive into the distinctions between the various kinds of businesses you may want to form, let's quickly get some terminology out of the way. Because we'll be discussing both business and the law, there are words and phrases you may think are interchangeable (and often are in common conversation) but here they mean very specific things.

- **Person**: A specific legal entity under the law. Persons have various protections and rights. A person can refer to a "natural person", a type of business, or even a town or city in some cases.

- **Company**: In the United States, a company is simply a group of persons doing business together. Some companies are legal entities, while others are just an informal group of people. This means that "forming a company" in the U.S. can be as simple as a group of friends deciding to go into business together and finding a name for the group. In the U.K. a company refers to a kind of specific, separate legal entity.

Hopefully this has cleared away some of the confusion and not replaced it with too much more. Now we're ready to dive in and discuss the different types of businesses in greater detail.

SOLE-PROPRIETORS AND GENERAL PARTNERSHIPS

Admittedly, I don't have a lot of experience running a sole-proprietorship or partnership so take this advice with a grain of salt. A sole-proprietor is "a type of enterprise that is owned and run by one person and in which there is no legal distinction between the owner and the business entity."[1] This means that you and your business are essentially the same thing from a legal perspective. By contrast, a General Partnership is "an arrangement where parties, known as business partners, agree to cooperate to advance their mutual interests."[2] Both of these arrangements can be formal or informal, in fact I've seen a Partnership sometimes described as, "what happens when two or more people decide to go into business together." If that sounds vague and informal, thats because it is.

If you and a friend decide to sell shirts together at a street fair, you've formed an implicit Partnership. Both a sole-proprietor and a partnership are business arrangements that don't form a legal entity in most cases. The people are the entities. By contrast, a Limited Liability Company (LLC) and a Corporation are formal and registered legal entities. A lot of small businesses you see around you day-to-day are sole-proprietorships or partnerships. They're easy to manage, easy to organize, with few legal responsibilities and the owner or owners file taxes in basically the same way they would normally. This simplicity probably sounds great, but there's a key downside to both of these types of businesses: they offer no legal protection and they draw very little distinction between what belongs to you (or your partners) and what belongs to your business. This means that lawsuits against your business can target your personal assets: your home, your car, etc. Herein lies the biggest downside with entity-less arrangements. Some businesses are able to purchase insurance or use other assurances like contracts to ensure they won't be sued by their customers or clients, but Web based businesses typically need a bit more protection than that.

CORPORATIONS

A corporation is a formal organization, registered with the state, that acts as a single entity. Perhaps un-intuitively, corporations can have only one member. One can think of different business types falling somewhere on a sliding scale. This scale ranges from easy to set-up and administer but difficult to expand, versus complex initially but easier to scale up to a large operation. Sole-proprietorships and partners fall closer to the first end of that spectrum, while corporations are closer to the other. While there are a multitude of different types of corporations, they each share a few key aspects: they are considered a separate legal entity or "legal person", they file taxes as themselves, and they offer protection for and distinction from those who own the corporation. Just like a real person, or "natural person" as the law calls them, a corporation can own things and make purchases. This means that when a corporation is sued, and damages are awarded, the lawsuit can only target assets owned by the corporation not by the owners personally. This distinguishes them from the two business arrangements we've already covered. Make no mistake though, this protection doesn't come free. There are tradeoffs to forming a corporation, and depending on the goal you have for your business, some are beneficial, and some may be considerable overkill.

In my opinion, there's only one reason that a person reading this book would want to form a corporation: they want to offer or sell stock. Some corporations can sell stock or ownership in the corporation, which can be an incredible asset. Once you form your corporation, you'll decide how much initial stock to offer. This number is all you'll ever have (assuming you don't split the stock later on), and you can sell this stock to buyers to raise money for your company. You can also give stock to people as payment for joining your company. This may sound great, (after all you can sell the stock for whatever people will pay and you can use that money to get your company off the ground), but be careful, stock aren't free. Those who own stock are part owners of the corporation, and they get to influence how the company is run proportionally to the amount of stock they possess. Effectively, the moment you sell stock in your corporation, that corporation is no longer yours: it's now jointly owned by everyone who owns stock. Those who own stock (the shareholders) typically don't manage the company directly, "shareholders instead elect or appoint a board of directors to control the corporation in a fiduciary capacity. In most circumstances, a shareholder may also serve as a director or officer of a corporation."[3] Lets unpack that statement a bit. Corporations are usually required to create a board of directors. Those directors are required by law to run the company in a way that benefits the shareholders. Directors then appoint or elect officers to run the company (i.e. the Chief Executive Officer or CEO).

If all this sounds like a lot of complicated legal stuff, that's probably because you're not looking to form a corporation. From my experience forming and managing a corporation is a lot of work, especially for a small team and even more so for a single person. If you're looking to build a long-term, profitable business for yourself or a small team, but you aren't planning to go public on the stock market or apply for Venture Capital, then you probably don't want to form a corporation. Luckily, there's one more option to discuss.

LIMITED LIABILITY COMPANIES

If you're feeling overwhelmed right now, that's ok. I promise that things will get easier from this point forward. It's important to understand the differences between formal legal entities like corporations and informal sole-proprietorships and partnerships because they both have significant drawbacks. On the one hand, a single-person, or a group of co-founders don't need to take on the burden and the complexity inherent in a corporation. On the other hand, the informality inherent in a sole-proprietorship or partnership doesn't provide the legal protection needed to do business on the Web and interact with customers and users from potentially all over the world. That's where the LLC, or limited liability company, comes in.

In the United States, a Limited Liability Company is a type of hybrid business organization that "combine[s] the pass-through taxation of a partnership or sole proprietorship with the limited liability of a corporation."[4] Just as their name implies LLCs aren't corporations, they're companies. This means that they aren't required to do a lot of the things that corporations are. They aren't required to have a board of directors, they are subject to far fewer laws and regulations, and they require far less administrative and record-keeping overhead. That said, LLCs can't issue stock in the traditional way and therefore LLCs have a much harder time applying for Venture Capital or other Silicon Valley investment staples. One particular benefit of LLCs is that, in most cases, they're taxed using a pass-through model. This means that you don't need to file taxes separately for your small business. Instead, you include your share of the LLCs profits and losses on your own personal taxes. This makes administering an LLC significantly easier than the alternative. LLCs are by far the most flexible option for small and medium businesses.

Like a corporation, LLCs are usually required to have a method to their madness. For LLCs this is called the "operating agreement". This agreement simply describes the formula by which your company is organized. In a larger company, this would lay out the process by which your company distributes profits and losses, votes on decisions, etc. You can think of this as your company's constitution. Once all of the LLC's members sign it, that agreement becomes a contract each member is legally bound to uphold. In some states, LLCs are required to have a written copy of this document, in others the requirement is far less restrictive. Either way, drafting an operating agreement is an important step. For multi-member LLCs, the agreement shapes your arrangement, duties, and roles. For a single-member LLC, the agreement distinguishes your company from you personally. Without one, your LLC may not be considered legally distinct from yourself and the protections it offers will evaporate. There are plenty of free templates online for various kinds of operating agreements. Don't worry too much about the legalese. While the operating agreement is a formal contract, as a single-member LLC your goal is to draw a line between yourself and your business, and remember, you can always alter the agreement as time goes on and your business changes.

LOCATING YOUR BUSINESS

This section might be a bit confusing and incredibly intimidating, so let's get some basics out of the way first. When you go to "organize" your LLC (i.e. start it up), you can do so in basically any state you want, even if you don't live there. This might sound strange, but there are reasons why some companies do this. The state of Delaware, for example, has a set of principles and precedent in its courts that favor corporations and companies in lawsuits, so, the thinking goes, if your company is in Delaware and you're under their jurisdiction, you're more likely to get a favorable outcome from any lawsuits you find yourself in. Lots of companies do this. By some estimates there are thousands of companies headquartered in Delaware that have no physical presence in the state. As someone who lives in California, and who's started LLCs in both Delaware and in California, I recognize the benefits this tactic might hold, but I wholeheartedly believe that organizing in another state is a waste of time and effort for a company of the size we're discussing. In my opinion, a single-member LLC that ships independent software is, realistically, never going to need the slight tactical advantage provided by this convoluted approach. Especially in California, where even "foreign entities" (which includes companies from other states) have to pay the yearly Franchise Tax anyway, organizing in Delaware just increases the administrative burden you'll have to bear. Unless your state has some really onerous law or business-hostile court system, just start your company in your home state; it's so much easier. The protections that an LLC grants will likely already be sufficient for a single independent software developer or small team. Engaging in weird corporate jurisdiction shenanigans just isn't going to help you at this scale. If your business becomes insanely profitable and your dedicated, full-time legal team tells you it would save your company money to relocate to Delaware, then by all means go for it. To be honest, that would be a great problem to have.

GENERAL ADVICE FOR BUSINESS OWNERS

No matter what kind of business you end up starting, or how you conduct it, you'll want to make sure you keep your business distinct from yourself. Not only is this good practice that generally makes accounting easier, it's often required. When conducting business, registering accounts, and contacting others for business purposes, use a dedicated email address that isn't tied to you personally. If you own a domain for your business (which you absolutely should), then you can set up an email address under that domain. Obviously you can use a variety of email addresses, and if you control the domain you can often create as many as you like. Personally, I prefer to have one email address for outward facing communications, one for company accounts, and one for me as an individual (just like the email you would get if you worked for the company). This not only confers an air of professionalism, it keeps your business and personal communications separate and distinct. You can easily identify what communications are on behalf of your business and which aren't. You can more easily track receipts, and more easily track legal financial transactions.

Additionally, you should separate your finances from your business, even if you run a sole-proprietorship. Separating yourself this way is convenient (once it's set up), and it's also often a requirement. Setting up a separate account is a pain the first time, and for some entities it can require applications and other paperwork. Depending on your needs, you may also want to apply for a business credit card. Banks will usually grant low-limit cards to indie-dev companies. These cards allow your business to build credit and consolidate expenses. As a software business, it's not likely that you'll need a massive extension of credit to buy a building or an expensive oven, instead you're looking to pay for some inexpensive services while separating your personal expenses from business expenses. Some banks will conduct an interview with you to determine how much credit they are willing to extend, but in most cases, even the smallest credit limit is probably enough for your needs.

Aside from the simplicity of accounting, separating yourself from your business has a legal benefit as well. In some cases, like with LLCs and Corporations, businesses are sometimes determined to be invalid if the owner or owners don't make the case that they are legally distinct from their company. Remember, by forming a legal entity, you're claiming that you are not the company and that your company is not you. You're arguing that you are distinct entities and should be treated as such. If you share the same email address, the same bank account, and the same credit card, that case becomes a lot harder to make. Don't worry too much about accidental purchases using your personal account. These rules are not all-or-nothing. Just make sure that the vast majority of your business is conducted in dedicated accounts and that any accidental purchases or subscriptions are explicitly reimbursed by the company to you or vice versa. Everybody accidentally buys something with the wrong account at least once. Just make sure you pay yourself back and keep track of those accidental purchases somewhere so you can remember them later.

Developing Your Ideas

You may already have an idea for the product or service you want your business to offer. If you do, then this chapter will give you the tools to sharpen and hone that idea into something marketable. If you don't, this chapter should help you develop a better intuition around what makes a good product or service, and hopefully give you a starting point. A lot of first-time founders and developers will start with a vague idea and jump straight into programming without thinking through the business side of things. This is a natural urge for technical people. In my experience, it's much more fun to write code and design websites than write business plans. Suppress this urge if you can. While a lot of your business plan can be decided organically as you go, there are a few things you really need up front. Without a solid plan, or at least the foundations of one, your development can slowly drift further and further from your intended goal. When it's finished you may be shocked to discover that your software has evolved into a behemoth, chock-full of unrelated features. This lack of focus and clarity is more than just a problem for you and your development further down the line. A lack of focus makes it harder for your customers to understand what your software actually does, how it improves their lives, and why they'd pay money for it. An up-front business plan (even one with very little detail) will offer potential customers a better understanding of what your software does, and support your claims of the value that it adds.

To that end, we'll spend the next few sections diving into what makes a good product or service, what features are required for launch, how to develop a roadmap, and how to price your features in a way that provides utility for your users and makes money for your business.

PRODUCTS VS. SERVICES

Software comes in a myriad of forms and each have their own benefits and drawbacks, as well as different reasons for their pricing models. Software as a Service is distinct from Software as a Product. SaaP is a more traditional way of selling software, and works best for compiled binaries, apps from an App Store, or large and expensive professional software. Software as a Product is purchased by the user in a one-time transaction, and updates may be free or require another purchase. Software as a Service, on the other hand, charges a recurring fee to access and use the software. The subscriptions vary but they could last for days, months, or even years. Netflix, Amazon Prime, Apple Music, and Microsoft Office are examples of companies selling their Software as a Service. Services are useful to businesses because they allow them to accumulate recurring revenue to cover recurring costs. Compiled binaries don't cost the business anything extra, no matter how often the customer uses the software, whereas web software requires servers and infrastructure to be running 24/7 to provide access to its users. As more software moved to the Web, businesses required a better payment model to address these ongoing overhead costs than a simple one-time purchase.

Stuart Hall famously performed what he called his "App Store Experiment" in 2013.[5] Starting in May of that year, hall released a small app on the iOS App Store and tried, in secret, a number of different pricing models and promotional strategies to compare their impacts and their ability to generate continual revenue.

> I wanted to build an app in one night, not tell a single person about it and run some experiments on it to see if I could get it to some level of success. I thought maybe I could get a few thousand downloads and make a couple of hundred bucks.

An App Store Experiment: Part 1, by Stuart Hall

In what has become a rather famous experiment in the iOS development community, Hall found that changes to his app's pricing model had the same, if not substantially larger, impact on his app's overall revenue performance compared with any other improvement he made to the app or its functionality. In short, his pricing model determined how much revenue he made as much or more than his feature-set. These days, pay-up-front apps are fairly rare and customers expect to at least be able to try a native app before spending any money. This is true in my own experience as well. Initially, Pine.blog did not offer a free trial and expected users to pay a $5 fee each month right away. This resulted in very few signups in the first months after the service went live. While the economics of Web services and mobile apps are substantially different, they do share similarities when it comes to what users expect an app or service to cost. In his experiment, Hall started with a paid-up-front app and gradually migrated to different payment systems. He experimented with making his app free, with adding one-time purchases for different features, with various types of subscription models, and much more. Overall, he found that the models that worked best, rather understandably, gave the users the most choice and the most flexibility. Users expect a free trial and they expect monthly fees to come with additional features.

While a lot of user expectations of software pricing are counter-productive in many ways, these expectations shape the market you're trying to enter. In some cases, your app can steer or shun the prevailing winds, the trends in a market, but to do so is to enter into a battle you'll always be fighting. Trying to convince customers to adopt an older and outdated but profitable business model may not be within your power. Lots of developers want to price their software in older, or more outdated ways. Developers would love to be able to charge $9.99 for a note-taking app up-front like they did in the old-days of the App Store, but customers have moved on. Pricing models, just like UI Design trends change and they evolve. You and your business must evolve with them. In most cases, it's easier to find a way to be profitable with the constraints you have, rather than pine for newer or less restrictive ones. Your pricing model is just another feature of your software. If you find that your users prefer a given pricing model over another, consider changing it. For what it's worth, Pine.blog's pricing model has changed three times thus far and I can't imagine that it will stay the same for its entire future.

WHAT MAKES A GOOD SERVICE?

Even though, in many respects, users are technically paying for access and to keep the service up and running, users still expect additional ongoing benefits to justify the monthly subscription. Simply keeping the lights on is often not enough. Keep this in mind during later chapters when we discuss pricing models and subscription tiers. Users should always feel that they're getting something for their money every month. For example, if your idea is for some sort of productivity tool, then you should make sure that the tool provides some periodic return. Companies like Netflix and Amazon Prime charge for continually updated content, and while that's an option you could consider, creating and hosting custom content can be difficult and time-consuming for a small business. Some services are effectively, what I would affectionately call, a CMS as a Service. They provide the ability for users to upload their own content to the service and view it across multiple devices. They are digital storage lockers in the cloud. In this case, the monthly cost is based on whether the user can access their own content and potentially share it with others. These kinds of services can be tricky to get right. In effect, the user is giving you their data and then paying you so that you won't lock them out of it. Each type of software service has different benefits and drawbacks, and depending on what kind of service you want to build, your pricing model and feature design will drive how users will justify paying for it.

Build What You'd Use

One of the easiest ways to determine whether a given service is valuable to users—and honestly, to ensure that you'll keep working on it—is if you'd find it useful yourself. Building something you want or need can be a very effective strategy. Market research is important (since that specific combination of features at a given price may already exist), but if you do find a gap in the market for a service you would be willing to pay money for, then you're off to a good start. If you've shopped around for alternatives already, your own desires and expectations of a service can inform what you think others would pay for a given feature-set. This can help you make decisions regarding your pricing model, product-roadmap, and even marketing strategy later on. If you can confidently claim that large numbers of people besides you would also pay for this software, even better. Also, as I just mentioned, building something you would want to use means that you have a vested interest in finishing it. If you want the software because it solves a problem in your own life, then that will drive you to complete it, or at least get it to a usable state. Motivation is key.

Be careful though. Just because you want a given software service to exist, doesn't mean that enough people want it to sustain your business. Services with small markets require higher prices to be viable, and if that service isn't worth the price needed to sustain it, people won't sign up, and your service will fail. In later sections we'll discuss how to conduct market research, estimate your market's size, and appropriately price your software. For now, realize that your intuition can be a helpful guide to what might be a good software service, but also keep in mind that you are definitely biased in this situation. You have a vested interest in the outcome of the service, and you are the kind of person with the skills, experience, and financial freedom to develop a side-business. You are unlikely to be a completely impartial judge or an accurate representative of the average software user.

MARKET RESEARCH

After you've developed the basic idea of what your service will do and what niche it's trying to fill, it's time for you to do some market research. This step is critical to determining the viability of your product or service, but if you're anything like me, it's an unenjoyable part of the process. Market research basically means scouring the Web for products and services that already fill similar roles. When you're conducting market research, you're aiming to answer a few basic questions:

1. What is the approximate size of the given market you're trying to enter?

2. What other products or services fill the same or similar niche?

3. What do they cost and what features do they provide for that cost?

4. How many competitors do you have that are on the market today?

5. How is your product or service different from theirs? Why would someone choose yours over another?

6. What kinds of users are being targeted by the existing solutions? Are you targeting the same, similar, or different users?

These questions are not only critical in determining whether your idea will be viable, but they can also assist in focusing your product towards fulfilling the needs of underserved or unserved groups rather than targeting users already covered by existing solutions. Maybe your solution is simpler, cleaner, and less expensive, or perhaps it combines multiple solutions or tools in a unique way, or maybe your product or service is just plain easier to use. Differentiating yourself doesn't mean being radically novel or require completely reimagining a given paradigm. It just means that you are unique in some way; you can stand out in a crowd.

Many of these questions will be difficult to answer, and some are impossible to answer with a high degree of certainty. Consider the question about market size. The point of this question isn't to force you to conduct months or years of research into the exact population of a given market. Instead, the goal is to give you a general idea of the size of your potential audience. If you're targeting a population that you estimate to be roughly 10,000 people in the U.S., you may wish to broaden your appeal (or charge more for the service). You can never assume you'll capture even 1% of a given market. So if you can't be profitable with less than 1%, it's time to rethink your strategy.

Let these questions guide your thought process and lead you to a more focused product or service. There's a reason that businesses, from publishing to venture capital, ask applicants to answer similar questions. As a business owner, you need to know why your idea has appeal or value, and be able to estimate approximately how many people would want it and what they would pay for it. Then, and only then, begin building.

OPEN STANDARDS AND INTEROPERABILITY

The Web is full of standards that significantly impact how we use different products and how those products interact, even if most users are completely unaware of their effects. Adopting relevant standards can allow your users to add more functionality to your service, access your service across multiple devices and platforms, and even allow other services to access your data on the user's behalf. This is an incredible competitive advantage, and studies have shown that software companies that adopt and participate in Open Standard use and development are more successful.[6] Most services and products are ignorant of the possibilities that are inherent in these standards and that gives you an edge. Take the time to research and become aware of different standards that govern the kind of service or product you're trying to build.

The blogging community is a poster-child for the power of the Web's open standards. Blogs have standards for feeds: RSS, Atom, or JSON feeds allow sites and tools to follow updates from the user's blog, standards like Webmentions and microformats allow for rich interactions between sites like comments, likes, and reposts, and, on the older side, the Meta-Weblog API specification allows apps and sites to post to a user's blog, freeing them to use whatever tools they prefer to write their posts. Blogging services that support these standards fit in with the community at large and encourage more development of these same extensions. This, in turn, makes the whole blogging community better. By adopting your community's standards, by becoming a potential community model, everyone benefits.

WEARING LOTS OF HATS

As a business owner you have a lot of different responsibilities, and as a one-person business you have even more. From day to day you will find yourself conducting market research, developing your user interface, optimizing your database, managing customer support emails, and doing your taxes. Balancing each of these responsibilities is hard and switching between them quickly is even more challenging. You may find yourself getting overwhelmed by all of the tasks on your plate at any given time. This is normal, but that doesn't mean it has to be. In this section, we'll consider how to manage each of the different responsibilities you have, how to balance both technical and business aspects, and how to keep yourself from getting distracted and overwhelmed by the multitude of decisions necessary for your business and your products. We need to define each set of responsibilities, each mindset, and give it a name. We'll also need some hats.

Discussing the different mindsets you need to inhabit can get weird, but luckily, there's already a good metaphor from the business world and it involves hats. At any given time, we wear a single hat, but we own far more than just one. In one day you might switch between your parenting hat, your Mac user hat, your Baseball coach hat (etc), maybe even multiple times. Putting on a new hat can shift your perspective on a topic or issue. For example, Apple may announce a new version of macOS with a feature you really wanted as an Apple User, but they may lock down a certain developer feature you depend on. If you put on your Apple User hat, this new release is a great improvement, but when you put on your Developer hat you may not be so optimistic about Apple's direction. Without thinking, we switch between these hats, these mindsets. In product development, as well as in life, separating out and categorizing the perspectives of each of these different versions of yourself can be incredibly helpful to clarify your thoughts on a topic. You may have concerns about a topic when wearing one hat (even if it is not your favorite hat or the most important to you) that you would not think about normally.

If any of this seems hard to grasp or unclear, think of yourself at any given moment as pretending to be one member of a large business that builds software. This type of business will have (among other things) customers, marketers, developers, product managers, accountants, sysadmins, designers, and customer support staff. When you're designing a feature, you're wearing your product designer hat, but you may need to get feedback from the developers to see how difficult they think the feature would be to implement. When you're thinking of developing a user interface you're wearing your developer/UI designer hat. In this role, you may also want to think about how easy it would be for the marketing department to sell this feature. When you're dreaming of new ideas, once again as a product designer, you may still be considering the financial implications as well: could you sell this feature and for how much? Each of these hats has its own perspective on the product and its own priorities. They want different things and it's your job to navigate each perspective and negotiate a compromise that best suits the needs of your business. You may have already experienced these different mindsets competing in your brain. If you've ever wanted a feature to exist in your software, but you struggled to summon the energy to actually build it, you've experienced a struggle between yourself as a product designer and as an engineer. With all that in mind, let's turn back to building software and look at which hats you'll need to wear and what each of them brings to the table. All of these different hats are important, but not all of them are equally important.

Thinking Like a User

When setting out to launch a product for the first time, it's typical for everyone involved to think like a user of this future product. Most of us spend our time as users of products and services, and even the most productive among us use software more often than we build it. As a user, we think about what would best suit our needs, what features are missing, and what would make our lives easier. This mindset trains our brains to think about tweaks, enhancements, and sometimes niche extensions of existing functionality. This mentality can be useful, but also dangerous on its own. Users don't often consider how a business with such features would support itself, how it would maintain and extend those features, and how much they'd pay for them. Thinking like a user is a good way to approach some aspects of product design (especially when it comes to ease-of-use and marketability) but you'll need to develop a few other head-spaces in order to ensure that your service can meet the needs of not just your users, but also the needs of your business and your development team (you).

Thinking Like a Product Designer

For our purposes, a Product Designer reviews both user feedback and the company's business goals, then they design the features that best fit the product and fulfill the given need. Not all features chosen by the Product Designer will be implemented, in fact most probably won't be. Product Designer is one of the most fun hats to wear. Free from technical implementation concerns and with just the goal in mind, your job is to dream of the possibilities. Passionate and creative Founders will spend a lot of time wearing this hat, especially in the early days of a project before everything is tampered down by the constraints of reality. When you're in this headspace there are almost no limitations on what you can and should consider. Looking for more customers? Why not try features targeted for the live streaming community? Looking to break into a new class of users? How about pivoting to support blogging? The possibilities are endless.

Of course, these dreams aren't all going to come true, but giving yourself the space to dream big and to be creative can be really helpful, whether you're stuck and floundering for what to do next, or you've hit a rough patch and can't seem to push forward. The trick is to not sell yourself too hard on the fantasy you're creating in your mind. Grand visions can help guide you towards a successful outcome, but keep in mind that the product or service may look completely different from the original vision by the time you launch. Once you've dreamt up a new vision and gotten CEO approval (more on that later) you should focus hard on what your current goals are and what's coming in the near future. Working on developing small, incremental changes will bring your product gradually closer towards that grand vision, allowing you to prioritize the most important aspects. For example, if breaking into the live streaming community is a goal worth pursuing, then perhaps adding features to your live chat should take precedence over other features in the pipeline. Your goal in this role is two-fold: dream big, then design features and improvements to start achieving that dream bit by bit. You can do this by thinking about specific Use Cases (though not in the strict Agile sense). What kinds of uses will your service support, and what features will enable your users to fulfill that Use Case?

As a Product Designer, you'll need to imagine your User Base. Products are rarely targeted at literally everyone. Who do you imagine will find your software useful? What's their demographic, their age group, their approximate income level, their education level, their job or industry, and their computer literacy level? This isn't to profile your users, but to guide you in making your product accessible to the widest range of your potential User Base. There will probably be multiple overlapping groups you wish to target. You may be attempting to reach both highly-paid computer-literate lawyers in major cities and lower-income rural drug store owners with spotty internet connections. These groups are sometimes referred to as Customer Segments. They're groups of potential users who you can explicitly make a case for why they would use your product. These Customer

Segments don't have to be super specific. For example, you could say you're targeting owners of Facebook Groups, or political activists on Twitter. Use these segments. How and why would they use this service? Try to imagine, or better yet just ask them. What features would be a nice to have versus what features would be crucial for them to adopt your software? Designing applicable Use Cases that reflect the actual needs of potential users becomes far easier when you have identified your Customer Segments, regardless of their size or composition.

Thinking Like a Developer

Just like the Product Designer hat from before, the Developer hat is a bit of a catch-all. It refers to basically everything technical whether that's development, architecture, system administration, networking, or security. In short, the goal of our Developer hat is to make the dreams of the Product Designer and the CEO come to life. This is where the magic happens, but it's also where you will need to set boundaries for yourself, and realistically manage the expectations created when you were in your other roles. The other hats aren't as concerned with technical complexity when making their decisions, which is a good thing because it allows them to imagine a future for the software that is unburdened by the harsh logistical reality of implementation. They instead focus more on the business and user satisfaction sides of the conversation. As a Developer, your job will be to listen to those other hats, then focus on the features that can actually be designed and implemented in a reasonable fashion and push back on those that can't.

Thinking Like a CEO

With every company and every project there's got to be a person (or a group of persons) with the ability and power to make decisions. They will be making the final call on whether or not a feature goes into development, if a pricing increase is justified, or if the marketing plan is ready for launch. This is the role we'll call CEO. When you're wearing this hat, your primary job isn't to dream of features or to decide what's best technically, your job is to keep your company going, and to keep the other hats employed. What's best for the product is decided by another person wearing another hat, your job is to decide what's best for the company as a whole. That could mean pivoting to another product, not implementing a needed refactor, changing the pricing model, or dumping the current marketing strategy. Each of these decisions could directly override the wants of a given team member. But remember, to the CEO these wants are only recommendations.

This sounds a bit dictatorial, and in a way it is. Regardless of the size of the company, a CEO should try their best to hear the concerns of others, understand the varying perspectives of their team members, and recognize their abilities and how they contribute to the company's product and services. But at the end of the day, a truly good CEO has to put the success and the continuation of the company itself before anything else. It is their job to make the final call. Sometimes this is easy, but other times it's very much not. When you are both the CEO and the Developer, you might find it hard to make difficult decisions. As a developer, you might prefer to build cool new tools or refactor old code than ship a release, but the CEO makes that call, not the Developer.

Additionally, it's job as the CEO to decide what features will actually make it into each launch, and that may go against the original launch plans created by the Product Designer. It's your job to set the overall strategic roadmap, the deadlines, and to decide if the service or product is ready for prime-time when that launch date arrives. You are the one making sure that the other members of the team are held accountable to the set dates, and it's ultimately on you to decide when to stop pursuing a given goal because it has become too costly. If you've had similar past employment experiences as myself, you may have had conversations with a boss where they made the final decision to either develop a feature 'The Right Way' or 'The Quick Way'. As CEO, you will be the one who has to make that call, and trust me, having that argument with yourself is no less frustrating.

Why All These Hats?

It probably sounds weird to describe a single-person business this way, after all no one expects you to actually argue with yourself in a conference room downtown. However, learning to think in these different ways prevents you from having to consider all aspects of a decision at once, which can quickly become overwhelming. You're training yourself to, at any given time, focus on a single set of constraints and goals, and afterwards seek help from others in your organization (yourself). This process can also train you to better understand why certain features are more important than others. A feature that's fun and exciting to build or design may have little business impact, which reduces the priority of the task. Left to our own devices, fledgling founders will often chase the fun and shiny things, leaving the real work undone.

PRICING TIERS AND FULFILLMENT-DRIVEN UPGRADES

When considering possible pricing tier options for your project, you may decide that your service will have multiple paid tiers of features, or even just a free tier and a paid one. Each tier should genuinely fulfill a given need the user may have. Your goal in constructing tiers isn't to up-sell your customers to the highest tier. Instead it's to convince the customer to pay as much as they can for the features that fulfill their need, without giving the customer the impression that you are taking advantage of them. Potential customers can be easily dissuaded from signing up at all if they feel that a service would be too expensive for their use case. In this example, too expensive doesn't necessarily correspond to how much each tier actually costs, but instead how much that tier costs relative to the features provided.

As an example, let's pretend that your service offers cloud photo and video storage. Customers upload their photos and videos to your service and you provide an app and website to access and share them. Take a look at the following tiers below:

	Basic	Premium	Deluxe
Photos Storage	500 MB	1 GB	500 GB
Video Storage	500 MB	2 GB	1 TB
Price	Free	$2/month	$50/month

In this rather extreme example, most paying users with a modern smartphone or camera would quickly exhaust the Premium tier limits. Those limits are well below other competitive services, and give the impression that the company is trying to force people to upgrade to a much more expensive plan even if they'd only want to upload a few gigabytes of content. Most users would see this pricing plan and feel cheated. They'd want a tier in the middle to bridge the gap. Also, because the Basic free tier and the Premium paid tier are so similar, most users would likely stick to their free plan instead of upgrading. Even though the Premium tier plan is relatively inexpensive, the upgrade is so limited that it would hardly be worth the effort. With this type of pricing structure, it's likely that users would feel that the goal of the service is to get them to spend $50 per month, not to best accommodate their needs.

When constructing pricing tiers, think instead about what the common use cases are that you're trying to address. Break those use-cases into groups based on common factors, and construct your pricing tiers around those groups. To continue with our previous example, our cloud photo/video service supports both uploading content for private browsing, and sharing that content with others perhaps via a gallery or blog. These are two different groups of features. Users who want to upload and organize their media for their own private collections will not necessarily require additional features that enable sharing, while users who do want to share content will need the same features as the collectors plus additional features as well. The tiers for this service now begin to emerge naturally. To share photos, users must already have uploaded and organized them, but the reverse is not true. Consider these tiers:

	Basic	Premium	Deluxe
Private Gallery	✓ (1 GB)	✓ (100 GB)	✓ (1 TB)
Public Gallery	No	No	Yes
Price	Free	$5/month	$10/month

What we've effectively done is create pricing tiers based on different segments of our user-base. Now there are options for users that wish to try out the service, users that just want to upload and store their photos in the cloud and access them anywhere, and users that want to share their collections with the world in a public gallery. This example demonstrates how to think about the basic structure and features of your software and how those can translate to pricing tiers.

Creating your pricing tiers based on use cases and the specific needs of your user base is a good place to start. If you are concerned about how to actually get users to switch tiers, there is a strategy I've employed previously that I've found critical for making customers happy and improving the conversion rate to the higher paying tiers. The limits imposed by the different tiers will most likely start off as fairly strict, clear limits. Like in the example above, users can't share photos unless they upgrade, but most people do want to share their photos with others in at least some rudimentary way beyond simply copy-pasting from your app or site, copying them to a flash drive, or (gasp) burning a CD. That doesn't mean you need to give everyone access to the Public Gallery features, instead you need to give your users a small taste of what it would be like to join the Deluxe tier. Allowing users in the Basic and Premium tiers very limited access to some sharing features accomplishes these two goals: the user has a better understanding of why they would want to upgrade, and the user doesn't feel like your app or site is a lacking or withholding a common feature. Perhaps Basic and Premium users can set a limited number of favorite photos to a public profile page, or send sharable links for individual photos to their friends and family. These features are separate, distinct, and far more restrictive than the customizable public galleries that the most dedicated users receive, but still allow the Basic and Premium users to see more of the service's potential and better understand the benefit of upgrading to the next level. This can be a great incentive for the users who find those particular features compelling.

Often times, and with our example above, tiers simply block access to a given feature unless users pay to unlock them. This can be an easy way to distinguish the tiers, and it can be easier to develop (which is an important factor). Other times services will distinguish between tiers not by limiting the number of features, but by adjusting how much access to those features a certain tier allows. We've already seen this with the storage limits in our example above, and services like Dropbox and Google Drive do essentially the same thing. In that prior example, a user may not need nor want any sharing features, but they might need more than 100GB of storage for their media collection. This structure provides two reasons to upgrade: access to sharing features, and increased storage limits. One tier is serving two different customer segments. Balancing your tiers well and layering multiple segments into a few tiers can be really powerful. It keeps the number of tiers low, which makes it easier for users to understand, and it helps convince users who are perhaps dedicated to a specific set of features to contribute more to support the service. As with many things though, be careful. Different overlapping tiers can become difficult to explain to users and may cause more confusion if they are too complex, or numerous. To combat this, you can use more descriptive names for the tiers, or even include a short description of the different features present for each tier. Take a look at our feature matrix again:

	Starter *Try it out!*	Collector *Organize your collection*	Photographer *Share with the world*
Private Gallery	✓ (1 GB)	✓ (100 GB)	✓ (1 TB)
Public Gallery	No	No	Yes
Price	Free	$5/month	$10/month

Each user that sees this list can now judge for themselves. Are they a collector trying to organize their many pictures or a photographer looking to get exposure? Lots of companies will title their highest tier something like "Pro" or "Enterprise" since they expect that the primary users of such a tier would be working professionals in a specific field, or looking to support an entire company on one account.

Pricing and Incurred Costs

In the examples above, the prices for each tier were more illustrative than actually useful. They don't account for things like bandwidth, or storage and hosting costs. When you're first developing the idea for your service, you may have a price range in mind, but before committing to that price you'll need to consider a few important factors. Namely, how much providing that service will cost, how many users will be required to break even, and how many users you'd need to turn a sizable profit. Each of these is a limitation that provides different challenges and require you to think about the future of your service. Hosting your service isn't free, and while the costs of hosting and bandwidth can increase as your service grows, there are fixed costs to getting everything off the ground in the first place. These costs, static and dynamic, are crucial to your calculations.

At first, when your service has just launched, the costs of the infrastructure will be more than you're making in revenue because you don't have any revenue. But, as long as you've planned things out accordingly, there is a threshold where the income from users will cover these expenses. This is the absolute minimum number of paying users you need to sustain the service, but possibly never have the money to improve it. After that is the number of users required to make a tidy profit. It's useful here to set goals, since the phrase "tidy profit" means different things to different people. Perhaps you'd like to earn an additional income to help with expenses, or maybe you're looking to make this a full-time gig. Either way, you'll need to calculate the number of paying users required to hit that limit. Tiered pricing schemes can make this harder to calculate, so you'll need to do some guesswork. Instead of total users, consider a value we'll call Average Expected Value (AEV). This is the average amount of income you expect to make from a given paying user. Let's look at an example to see how you can calculate this number using the tiers from before:

	Starter	Collector	Photographer
Price	Free	$5/month	$10/month

Let's say we're aiming for a conversion rate of 3% from users in the Starter Tier to one of the Paid Tiers, and we'd roughly expect about 20% of the paying users to be in the highest tier. That leaves us with the following AEV:

```
AEV = $5/month * 80% + $10 /month * 20% = $6/month
```

That's an average of $6 per month per paying user. Now, using the conversion rate from before and assuming we'd like to make a total of $5,000/month, let's calculate our total expected user-base.

```
N(users) = (Income / AEV) * (1 / Conversion Rate)

N(users) = ($5000 per month / $6 per paying user per month)
           * (1 / 0.03 paying users per total users)
         = ~27,778 total users (~834 paying users)
```

These initial numbers for the conversion rate and the tier breakdowns are estimates. As your service grows you'll be able to refine and recalculate these numbers, but for now this gives you a ballpark estimate.

Now let's look at your costs. The cloud can be notoriously difficult to price out in advance. The design of your system will have a huge impact on your costs, but once you have an outline of your system architecture (as long as you don't go too crazy with bleeding-edge cloud tooling), you'll be able to accurately estimate your monthly hosting and bandwidth costs. For the sake of example, let's say we did know our system architecture and we had chosen a hosting provider. We said before that we'd like to earn $5,000/month in revenue from our service, but our previous example is not taking cost into account. Here's a simple formula to help us calculate our costs, assuming we always use servers of the same size.

```
Expenses = (N(servers) * Server Cost)
           + (Required Storage GB * Storage Cost per GB)
           + Bandwidth
           + External Services (Texting, Email, etc)
```

For now, let's assume we've calculated our storage costs as $100/month for our initial launch and rollout. Using the num-

bers from our previous calculations, let's recalculate our required user-base.

N(users) = ((Profit + Expenses) / AEV) * (1 / Conv Rate)

N(users) = (($5000 + $100) / $6) * (1 / 0.03) = ~28,889

As you can see, our total required user-base just grew by over
a thousand users. Keeping your costs down is necessary to make
your new business profitable, so be careful when you're signing
up for a new service or platform, and be sure to include the expected costs you'll incur in your estimates.

Enterprise Based Tiers

Many companies price their products and services with enterprises in mind. Companies large enough to consider themselves an 'Enterprise' often require significantly larger limits and
more complex features than other individuals or small companies, therefore supporting Enterprise-level features is likely to
be challenging. It may be best to have an explicit enterprise tier
on which every limit, feature, and price in the matrix just says to
"Contact Support". If a large company does want to use your
service, they can explain their own needs and you can customize
a pricing model for their specific use cases. Because of this custom level of support, the cost of Enterprise software is often
much higher (even by an order of magnitude) than the normal
commercial solutions. A lot of consumer-focused companies
don't bother marketing themselves to Enterprises, and that's
fine, but if you believe that your software could be beneficial
and customizable, then it's good marketing to at least give companies the option to contact you for more information.

You can also structure your software to take advantage of the fact that Enterprises are usually large bureaucratic institutions that often have byzantine purchasing processes. While I have very little experience selling software to an enterprise, I've worked for large organizations before and have had to purchase a lot of software on behalf of the enterprise. Let's look at an example from the real world that explains how to easily sell your software to Enterprises without getting blindsided by their processes yourself.

In the Java world, a company called Redgate (a favorite of large businesses that call themselves Enterprises), sells a software product called Flyway that provides automatic database migrations and rollback support to Java applications. The product has three tiers: a free Community Edition, a paid Professional Edition, and an Enterprise Edition. In a clever bit of pricing and product tier design, a headlining feature of the Enterprise tier (aside from longer support guarantees) is the ability for customers to pay with a Purchase Order and opt-out of automatic billing renewal. These are classic Enterprise demands because of the nature of large business needs, but those additional limited features come at a substantial increase in cost.[7]

Enterprise software solutions can be useful for certain projects, and fairly lucrative for your business, but keep in mind the added income does require additional support and billing work from you.

THE MINIMUM VIABLE

Your initial launch is your chance to finally reveal your software to the world. It's an opportunity to generate buzz, get some users, and show off your ideas. Realistically, every feature you've wanted to build probably won't make it into the initial launch, so the question becomes: "What features do you launch with?" or more poignantly: "What features don't launch?" Making the decision to cut a given feature from the launch can be tough. Most founders and product-minded people want to deliver the best experience they can and show off the full potential of their idea. They don't want to cut anything. Everything, at least every major thing, must launch. I've been down this road myself with a few projects early on, and this situation is incredibly common common.

It'll launch when it's done. This seemingly commonsense statement conceals a dangerous paradox. One that lies not with the statement itself, but with who's saying it and what they mean by the word "done". To a lot of people, and arguably to developers in particular software is never done. It's always a work in progress, a thing that can be improved on, tweaked, made just a bit better, faster, cleaner, clearer, or more stable. To strive for the goal of product or service completion is akin to Zeno's Paradox: no matter how close you get, you never quite reach the finish line. Lots of projects die because of exactly this scenario. The founder or other core members are so caught up with whether their passion project is complete (which it never will be) that they just never launch. The project uses up its time, funding, or personnel and dies. Be wary of the this scenario; even the fastest group of developers and designers can't finish an infinite project.

The way around this is pretty simple, but may require a slight mindset adjustment. Instead of focusing on when a project is complete (which, as we've discussed, will never happen), focus on launching the bare minimum of what's required to fulfill the need.

ESTIMATING TIMELINES

Once you have a set of features laid out, you can start estimating just how long each one of them will take to develop and test. Timelines are notoriously hard to get right and there are legions of books about how best to estimate and improve your time estimation skills. Typical time estimation strategies center around a team of people and involve lots of explicit process. Since you don't have a team (or you have a very small one) a lot of those strategies can be complete overkill. Sprint planning, retrospectives, and story point estimation are common practices at modern software firms, and while they do have benefits, they can often hinder your work when your bandwidth is so incredibly limited. If you're trying to build a software company yourself, working only nights and weekends, it's hard to justify spending hours estimating the exact amount of work involved in building each feature.

Detailed time estimation and explicit processes are a bit like Calorie Counting to lose weight. I know this may sound strange, but as someone who's used Calorie Counting as a weight-management tool for years, I feel confident with this comparison. The goal of Calorie Counting is simple. Log everything you eat and drink, and count the calories. Set a daily calorie goal and stay below it. Sometimes called the Hacker Diet (though that name is applied to many diet trends these days that have nothing to do with Calorie Counting), this method can be incredibly effective, and also incredibly annoying as you have to count the exact calories in every chip you eat and every soda you drink. The main benefits of both Calorie Counting and explicit processes (time management tools like story points, retrospectives, sprint planning, and others) are related to how these processes retrain your brain to think differently about food (or time). You develop your intuition and train yourself to recognize large calorie foods and large effort tasks. Eventually you reach a point where you're able to 'guesstimate', with a fairly high degree of confidence, the number of calories in a food and how many calories you could still eat in a given day, just like you're able to eventually estimate how easily you could develop a given feature without going through a set explicit process.

If you are working on the project sporadically, like on nights and weekends, I don't recommend the use of absolute time like days, weeks, or months. Those time frames are too large to be accurate and, more importantly, they give you the wrong impression. If you estimate that a feature could be completed in five days, then you may make the mistake of claiming it will be completed by next week. This is a crucial fallacy. Using calendar time (days, months, weeks) may give you the impression that development will happen on a set schedule, but this is rarely the case, especially when moonlighting a project. If you typically work in short stints at night after work is done and kids are asleep, then the number of days you estimate is effectively worthless since you don't work in full-day increments. Instead measure the time in groups of hours, or what we'll call a session. The goal here is to estimate how many typical, uninterrupted sessions you'd need to finish a given feature. If you're working full-time on the project this could be measured in work days, but that can still get problematic. Here we'll define a session as four hours, but if you find that you can't set aside a dedicated four hour session, two hours will work just fine. The point here is not that the sessions are long, but that they are continuous. They should be your best guess as to how many dedicated hours you can go without being pulled into other things.

Once you've defined your session (which is effectively a crude story point for you scrum folks), use it to start estimating. Starting out, take your list of features and break them into logical groups; here we'll use Account Management, Payment Processing, Private Galleries, and Public Galleries as our broad groupings. These categories aren't really independent, after all you can't upload a photo to a gallery if you don't have an account, but for now we'll ignore that detail. Estimate each sub-bullet and sum them to get the total for the entire section. If you can, break the items in the list into smaller chunks, ideally one to two sessions long. Be sure to create tasks that are independent or largely isolated. After this step, you'll be left with a list of discrete, manageable tasks that can be done in one to two sessions. This serves two key purposes. The first is motivational; it feels good to finish something and that small dopamine hit can help keep you going. The second is more nuanced. When you only have a small chunk of time to work and those time periods are spread apart, it's easy to lose track of your progress, your thought process, and your specific investigation of the problem you're solving. It's common for developers to avoid distraction and to keep working on a problem simply because they're embedded in finding the solution. Stopping early could cause key insights to fade from memory and make it harder to pick up the problem later. Having to stop working in the middle of implementing a complex solution is incredibly disruptive because when you do get around to working again you may spend that whole session just catching yourself up to your previous position. Sometimes this can't be helped, especially with larger tasks, but avoiding it should be the goal.

Like most things in project management, time estimation isn't only a business tool. It can help you as a developer build better features, and feel more accomplished in doing so. Time estimation is a skill and it's one that only gets better with practice. It's never going to be perfect, so if you underestimate the effort required for a given feature, don't be too hard on yourself. When the feature is complete, take a look at the parts of the task that took longer, or that you'd missed entirely, when estimating. Use that experience to improve your time estimation skills the next time. Every release, from launch onward, is a chance to better test and refine your time estimation skills. As with most things, practice makes perfect, and you'll get a lot of practice.

Technical Considerations

Now that you have a better understanding of how to hone the idea for your business, it's time to dive into the first crucial set of decisions you'll need to make when building your product or service: you'll need to choose what tools you want to use. The software community is constantly discussing and debating what tools fledgling entrepreneurs should choose and even after all this debate there is almost no consistent, agreed upon answer. On sites like Hacker News, it seems like every week the set of recommended tech for a website or app has changed, and that the only way forward is to throw away everything from the past week's recommendations and start over. The best Web stack is dead, long live the best Web stack. This is, of course, completely ridiculous, and a result of the software community being a heterogeneous collection of developers with drastically different goals, methods, and starting conditions all forced into the same conversation. In reality, companies rarely if ever change their underlying technologies, and there's a good reason for that: there's no need. Many developers build software as a hobby. They explore new tech, and then they share their experiences and insights with the community. This appreciation for tinkering is part of what makes the software community great, but such advice is usually not useful to those starting a business. Building a hobby project is different from building a real product or service. Hobby projects are just that: hobbies. If they never launch, that's ok. If they serve no purpose, that's ok. If they're constantly half-working and mid-refactor, or even if they do nothing but teach the hobbyist new tech, that's ok too. However, when you're building a real product, those results are death sentences.

The technologies you choose should amplify your powers as a developer; they should make it easy to build and design new features, eliminate redundant or time-consuming work, and make it easy to do things quickly. Like most things, your technical choices affect your motivation. Being able to release frequent and fast updates is rewarding; getting stuck doing long and arduous tasks is not. In this section we'll look at how to choose technologies. We'll look at the criteria you should use to evaluate new tech, when to violate those rules, and what kinds of technologies you should avoid all together. Your technology should advance the interests of your company and your product, and you should choose technology that makes your users happy; it doesn't need to make you happy. Being able to ship features to happy users will do that on its own.

HOW TO CHOOSE TECHNOLOGIES

The tools you choose exist to make your life easier and increase your productivity, but they also serve as the primary form of technical debt, or cruft, in your software. Choosing the wrong tools can complicate your software with arcane anti-patterns, require constant upgrades and refactors with each breaking change, and expose your software to exploits if your tools haven't reached maturity. Shipping a product requires that you build features and squash bugs with your own code, not with someone else's. Tools and technologies that are raw and unfinished or unproven can often save you time up front, but cost you dearly later on. On the opposite front, old tools can often fall out of favor and become unsupported, or require arcane or ancient support libraries. You don't want to develop your project with technology that's one foot in the grave, but you also don't want to be anywhere near the bleeding edge. Whilst it may be more fun, and exciting to be walking that line, it's a line you'll always be chasing. More importantly, it's called the bleeding edge for a reason: it can hurt you.

Keep in mind that the criteria in this section are subjective. They have worked well for me and many others, but your preferences may vary. You may not give as much weight to some of these criteria or you may find that some are unreasonable for your problem domain. That's ok, but remember: each of these criteria exist for a reason. If you're going to replace one, you should figure out how to fill the gaps left behind. Adopting any tool carries some implicit risk. You're assuming that the tool will stay supported, receive bug fixes, and not simply vanish into the wind. Adopting a tool is an extension of trust. In today's world, developers usually need to incur some risk and use tools and software built by others in order to create something useful. These criteria do not eliminate the risks inherent in adopting technologies. They only seek to minimize that risk. There are lots of valid reasons why you'd choose to use tools that fail some or most of these criteria, but you need to consider the consequences and be sure that you're comfortable taking on that increase in risk. With all that in mind, let's now investigate each criteria in turn, and look at their advantages and disadvantages.

It Fulfills the Need

The tools you choose should fit the need you have. This may sound trite, but it is advice often overlooked. Never underestimate the allusive power of the Next Shiny Thing. If you're looking to build a mobile app, Web technology probably isn't the best place to start. Lots of tools are cross-platform, but often the best tool for the job is not. Take a look at the tools that developers in the space you are entering actually use, not what outsiders say they *should* use. Be careful to choose tools and approaches that fit your project's specific goals. If a platform encourages a certain code style, adopt it. You don't have the extra time to spend fighting against your tools, instead of shipping software.

It Is Familiar

Staying on top of new tools, frameworks, and libraries can be a full-time job and constantly learning new approaches to solving the same problems often leads to nothing getting solved at all. Applications, especially on the Web, do a very finite set of things: they collect data in a form, display information to a user, perform some kind of background processing, and occasionally send and receive requests to and from other applications. If you have a preferred set of tools to accomplish those tasks that you're familiar with, use them. There's no need to reinvent the wheel or relearn a methodology. Learning in general is an important part of being a developer, and it's often the most attractive part for some people. A lot of developers love to tinker and experiment with new ideas, new solutions, new approaches, and new tools. That kind of work can be extremely rewarding, but it can also doom a product and your company. During the course of forming your company, building your product, marketing your work, and setting up servers you're going to be learning a lot already. There's no need to pile on the additional work of relearning how to make websites. If you can, stick to what you know.

It Has Reached Maturity

Any software that powers the core of your product should be mature. Avoid using newly released or in-development software to power your commercial systems. Many first time entrepreneurs make the mistake of chasing the new hotness, and they build their software with the framework du-jour. It's an appealing trap to fall into. Newly released or in-dev tools often get a lot of press, they're discussed in forums, and they're the subject of talks at conferences. Blog posts from across the community will claim that the old ways are dead. They claim that everyone should switch to a new framework that's never been used outside of the group that built it to power systems its never been tested on. Don't do this.

Old, boring, and mature software is going to be your best bet, especially for constructing the core of your system. New kinds of databases and Web frameworks aren't worth investigating. They're fun to play with, but your goal is to ship software to customers, not play with new tools. Mature tools often have better documentation (which means it fits another of our criteria) and may even have a regular release cycle with Long Term Support (LTS) Releases. These releases have a longer timeframe during which they are actively supported. During this time, they receive security updates, and are usually guaranteed to work with more tools than a typical release. An example of a tool that has a reliable and dependable release cycle is the Django Web Framework for Python. New releases drop every six to eight months and go out of support in one year, but every third release is an LTS and is supported for three years.[8] This regular cycle dictates much of the culture surrounding the project. Plugins and add-ons march in lockstep with the latest LTS release, ensuring that the popular tools always work with the current supported versions, and like clockwork, when a release is no longer supported by the Django Software Foundation, most plugins drop support as well. The Django community changes regularly, like the seasons, ensuring new features are added and that everyone stays up to date, but also dropping support as needed. Developers using an LTS can set a reminder to upgrade their software over a year in advance, and all the while know that they'll get all the benefits of the regular security updates. By depending on stable and mature tools, you can rest assured that your software will keep working as expected. Don't underestimate the value of that kind of stability.

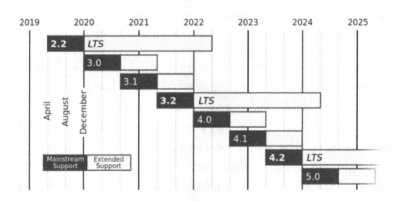

Django's Active Version Support Timeline

Javascript libraries like jQuery and lodash, Web frameworks like Django, Rails, and Flask, Linux Distros like CentOS, and databases like Postgres aren't flashy. They aren't "cool". But they work, and they work well. There are countless examples of trendy start-ups announcing that their world-changing technology is built on boring, reliable tools. Instagram and 23andMe are powered by Django. Hey, the newly-launched email service, runs on Rails and has no dynamic front-end at all. GoFundMe and Facebook use PHP, and Ebay and Netflix run on Java. Of course companies use a variety of tools, and some of those tools change over time, but while it's certainly the case that some or all of these companies use trendy languages and frameworks (Facebook using React is a great example), their core software is usually pretty unremarkable. That's both a good decision on their parts and, as we will see, it can be directly beneficial to you as well.

Mature tools are less likely to have critical bugs, short-sighted designs, frequent breaking releases, and other annoying or time-consuming problems. Mature tools get reliable security updates and have often been around long enough to have built up support infrastructure like foundations and funding to ensure they don't one day just vanish into the ether. Mature software is also accountable to large groups of people. In short: if you don't have the time or bandwidth to spend hours fixing your tools and instead, need to launch software, use mature tooling and avoid the Next Big Thing. You can always play with shiny new tools later after your business is doing well. By that time you'll even be getting paid to do so.

It Has a Substantial User Base

The size of a given software's user base is a good indicator of the stability and reliability of the software itself. You don't get to be popular by breaking everyone's code all the time (with the possible exceptions of Swift and React). You get to be popular by being reliable and focused. When investigating a tool or library, look for two specific callouts on the software's website: who sponsors the software and who uses it. If you see a library that is sponsored by Microsoft or used by Reddit, then it's pretty safe to consider adding that tool to your product as well. This isn't a perfect metric by any means, but it leads us to two key insights. When organizations choose to use a tool, even for an R&D project, and they inform the developers of the tool. This implies a sort of "Stamp of Approval" from that organization. When a large organization ships good software using a given tool, it gives the impression that others can use this tool to ship good software too. When Microsoft, Dropbox, or Instagram use a given tool, it means that the software can handle the complex use-cases those large organizations have. The software that those organizations build is probably substantially more complex than yours will be (especially at the beginning). When you're choosing tools, be sure that you're not going to be the biggest fish in the pond, or the largest and most significant user of the tool. By using the same tools as the big fish, you ride their coattails[9]. They push the limits of the framework or library, they find the bugs, and they have to fix them (or at least log them for others to fix). This means that you essentially leverage some of the work that these big organizations do, for free. If the tool works for them when their code is written by dozens of developers, running in disparate data-centers, handling a variety of complex use-cases, it'll likely work for you just fine. If you're the big fish, you have to do that work yourself.

Sponsorships likewise play a role in determining the quality of a given software. If multiple large organizations, or even lots of small organizations, use the software and are willing to sponsor its development, then that software is probably a good bet for you and your product. Organizations and individuals don't really sponsor bad software. Sponsorships ensure that a given software is going to stick around for a while. Open Source maintainers are often working on projects during off-hours, but paid maintainers can not only deliver more features on a more reliable schedule, their work tends to be of a higher quality as well. Paid maintainers are also less likely to simply burn out and abandon the project. This makes a lot of intuitive sense of course, but factors like this rarely make it into the calculations that developers, especially first time product developers, make when picking their tools.

It Is Under Active Development or Maintenance

Software, especially Open Source software, tends to evolve in a fairly typical manner. It follows one of three possible trajectories. The most common is the one we'll discuss the least: where a software either fails to launch or fails to become popular enough to ever find widespread use among the wider development community. This scenario accounts for the vast majority of software on the Web, and since the software never gains widespread adoption, that's all we'll say about it. The other two paths are more relevant to our goals here.

Both paths begin in the same place. Initially, a group decides to build a tool to solve a problem that they have. Over time the project grows and gains followers. During this phase, lots of exciting stuff happens. The software becomes stable. People start to rely on it. And then there's a fork in the road.

Along one path, the developer or developers continue to work on the project, the software evolves a stable if not frequent update cycle, and enters its maintenance phase. It goes on to become a staple of the community. After a while, it may no longer garner as much attention, but the software will settle into a stable rhythm. Use this kind of software if you can.

The second, and unfortunately more common, path breaks off from the first after the project gains popularity. One day, without notice, something happens. The maintainer steps away, either because of burnout, a personal lifestyle change, a toxic community, or lack of funds to continue. One day the repo is just dead. The author may publish a post-mortem on their reasons for abandoning the project and call for a maintainer to step into the newly formed gap. If a maintainer steps up, it can be the critical lifeline that pushes the project back into the prior scenario, but often times no one does and the project simply dies. It gets no further updates, no security patches, and no bug fixes. If large portions of your software depend on the abandoned tool, you may be forced to dedicate critical time to porting, replacing, or rewriting your product, and that is scant time you often can't afford early on. While it's essentially impossible to predict if this will happen to a project at some period in its lifetime, there are a multitude of warning signs to watch out for. Your goal should be to minimize the chances of this scenario happening to you. Before you simply install a library or decide to go all-in on a given framework or tool, check the commit history. Does this tool get at least occasional updates or patches? Activity doesn't need to be constant, but it should be relatively recent, preferably in the past six to eight months (though for smaller projects a year is probably fine). Some projects may be feature complete and will rarely see updates. This isn't necessarily a bad thing. Lower-level packages and support utilities often only change when the underlying language does and sometimes compiled binaries will continue to work for years after being built. The meaning of the term "recent updates" depends on the type of tool, the language it's written in, and the ecosystem it's a part of. Low-lying audio frameworks for example are less frequently updated than Javascript front-end frameworks for many reasons. Let this knowledge factor into what you consider "recent".

Sticking to tools that are robust, and under active development or maintenance, helps you avoid getting blindsided by events beyond your control. Seek out tools that have a proven track record of sticking around for the long haul. Minimize the possibility for other tools and frameworks to impact your business and take up your development time.

It Offers Wide Compatibility

Be sure that the tools you use are compatible with multiple different approaches and upstream tooling. Be skeptical about tools that require multiple layers in your software to be a certain way. Avoid web frameworks that only support a single kind of database, or API libraries that require certain companion libraries on both the front-end and back-end. These kinds of tools limit how your software can be changed and how the tool can be used for use-cases beyond what the developer intended.

On the other hand, tools with tight integrations can be simpler to set up and use. If you're unfamiliar with a given problem domain or solution, then it may be appealing to choose a tool that solves multiple issues across your software stack. These are calculated risks and can be worth taking, but in that case it's important to sketch out the boundaries for a given tool. Where does it fall short? If you needed to add a new feature, would you be forced to implement another solution, or could this one be adapted to support both features? Is there only one integration-of-record, or has the community not yet needed to implement a competitor to one portion of the tool? These questions and more can help you evaluate whether a limited tool can be useful to you. However, it can often just be easier to avoid these kinds of questions all together and choose tools that are limited in scope, or implement open standards that can be extended by others.

It Supports Multiple Use-Cases

Software that supports a wide variety of possible use-cases, that is general purpose tools, tend to be easier to source than specialized ones. The downside, of course, to this kind of software is that it may not be immediately obvious that it fills the need you have. What, after all, is the immediate value of a generic key-value database like Redis to your application? Specialized tools may seem like a safer bet. They often explicitly do what you need them to, and provide sensible defaults for quick and easy setup. The downsides, though, are hidden in the very thing that makes them useful. The more specialized a tool is, the more of them you need to fulfill a wide swath of use-cases. Adding specialized tools in the beginning can help you get up and running, true, but you pay for that easy setup later on when your software has grown beyond what that tool can provide. You're then left with the decision to either extend or migrate away from the tool to make it support more general use, or you can add more tooling. Extending software can be a worthwhile calculated risk, but migrating is hard, error prone, and delays new features. Adding more tooling only kicks the can further down the road and increases the surface area for this same situation to reoccur in the future. In general, you should avoid adding new tools. If the number of new packages and plugins grows with each new release of your product, you've probably

made some bad decisions. Obviously adding new features sometimes requires new tooling, but after a point your project should
hit an equilibrium. You'll find yourself tackling new facets of a
problem, not new problems entirely. Here's an example: if you
find yourself adding a live-chat feature to a standard Web Application, investigating Web Sockets and adding new tools for
handling them is natural and expected. However, you shouldn't
need to add new tooling if you're simply extending an existing
feature or adding more API endpoints. In that case, you already
have tools in place for the existing features that can accomplish
that goal. What makes these new extensions deserving of new
tooling?

Sometimes developers will add or migrate to new tools as
part of a new feature. It's not uncommon to move certain parts
of an application's infrastructure to a new framework or language under the hood during an otherwise mundane feature
addition. Try to avoid this tendency, especially before launch.
There is a valid set of reasons for migrating tools before launch,
but it's very, very short. Like I said, migrating is hard and you're
often left with a worse version of your app when it's done.

It Has Good Documentation and a Good Community

Good documentation is a bellwether for the quality of a given
software. Good documentation reflects the community that relies on it, and likewise bad documentation can reflect an apathy
or a lack of interest in a project. This isn't always the case however. In the real-world, simple, lower-level utilities are often really useful and poorly documented, while higher-level, more gen-
eralized tools are often better documented. Nevertheless, documentation can sometimes help you judge the tool itself, and
the community that uses it. There are multiple forms of docu-

mentation and they serve different uses. Code-level documentation in code comments can be helpful to contextualize why a give function works the way it does, but it's no substitute for browsable, searchable documentation on the Web. Documentation generation tools are really easy to integrate into most applications these days, so there's no excuse for poor or lackluster documentation in a modern library. The gold standard for documentation however, isn't code-level documentation focusing on method signatures and return types, it's User Guides. These guides explain more than just how to use the software. They cover why you should use it, and importantly, when you shouldn't.

User Guides come in many forms. Good User Guides explain more than just how to use a given tool. They explain the problem that the tool aims to solve, how it does so (including any misnomers, implementation quirks, and gotchas), and good documentation helps developers across various skill levels. There are lots of examples of great documentation out there, but let's look at three in particular: Django (the Python Web Framework), Postgres (the Open Source Database), and Linode (the Linux hosting provider). Each of these three examples have their own advantages and disadvantages, but the focus here will be not on the technical merit, but on their documentation.

Django is well known in the Python community for providing excellent documentation. Guides range from the typical Getting Started explanations to in-depth discussions about the tradeoffs of different kinds of database indexes and the security risks of different typical configurations. Similarly, Postgres' documentation provides examples of not just how to use Postgres and query the database, but also dives into how to perform routine backup/restore processes, how to maintain your database over time, and how to upgrade your database to new versions. In the hosting space, Linode and Digital Ocean provide excellent documentation and both have long been praised for helping sysadmins and developers with a variety of issues. Linode's excellent guide "Securing Your Server", guides sysadmins through the typical best practices of securing a Linux server on the Web.[10]

The documentation for a given software tends to directly relate to the quality of that software's community. Simplistically, a community is shaped by the people that actively participate in that community. There are countless examples of software communities with dismissive, rude, and intolerant members that make it difficult for outsiders to use or experiment with the tooling because they're afraid or unable to ask for help. Before adopting a major new tool, search around and get a feel for the kinds of discussions that the tool's community encourages. It often doesn't matter how useful a tool is if the people using it can't or won't help you when you have issues. Search out communities that foster new developers and try to avoid communities that punish them. It's not always possible, or even the best option, (especially if a given solution is leagues ahead of others) but it's nevertheless an important criteria to consider when adopting new technologies into your product.

It Is Open Source

A great deal of web software libraries are Open Source these days, especially in the communities of the Web's most popular languages. Simply being Open Source doesn't mean that a given software or library automatically checks this box, instead it's a suggestion that it may be worth further investigation.

Read the source code of software or libraries you intend to use. You don't need to read all of it like a novel, especially if you're unfamiliar with the language it's written in, but you should try to have at least a basic understanding of how your tools work. After all, it's just more source code and you're trusting that it functions properly. Reading source code, especially if it powers a critical framework or library your code depends on, is a really important step to evaluating the tool and its usefulness. If you're having trouble following the logical flow or understanding the terminology, that could be a sign that you either need more clarification about what this software does, or that it's over-designed and over-complicated. The Web especially is fairly straightforward: it's just text over a socket rendered in a browser. If your tools try to make this paradigm more complicated, then perhaps it's not worth your time. Clear, concise, and readable source code is critical and doubly so if the library has little-to-no documentation. As mentioned above, lacking good documentation is a warning that the project may not be as reliable as it seems, but lacking documentation is not a 100% make-or-break omission. Good source code can go a long way towards making up for a lack of good documentation, although it's never a complete substitute. Good source code can also help you identify and work around bugs in the framework or library.

When code is Open Source, you can learn from it. If you're building a custom extension to a feature in the library, or trying to save yourself time by building a few abstract or generic tools used throughout your product, it's best to build those tools and abstractions using in-context terminology, style, and conventions. You can often gain key insight into how the authors of the tool think about the given problem-domain by reading the source code, and their conventions and styles can often save you from headaches and pain-points that the authors are already working around in their designs.

Reading source code is time consuming, and does not need to be done all at once. You're not reading it for fun. You're reading it to expand your knowledge of the tool, its preferred uses, its shortcomings, and its design. Most developers don't take this step, either because it seems unnecessary or too time consuming, but you aren't trying to be like "Most Developers". Read the source code of others. It's easier to write good code when you know what it looks like.

WHEN TO USE IT ANYWAY

Sometimes a library won't fit one or most of the criteria laid out here, but it can still be the right choice to adopt it in your product. That's ok. Some problem-domains are too complex or unfamiliar to write yourself and it's possible that no better solutions exist or that the alternatives don't fit your needs. Assuming the risks inherent in your product is part of doing business and some things can't be avoided. Depending on which criteria are unsatisfied, there's a number of things you can do to help fill the gaps.

If the software is open source, but lacks active maintenance, or certain features you require for your product: fork it. Forking open source projects and maintaining a separate, custom version just for you is a completely reasonable strategy. Using the software directly means that it could be altered and introduce breaking changes unexpectedly. This is especially true if the software lacks a release schedule, hasn't reached a stable version yet, or isn't under active development. Forking ensures that the only changes that make it into your main codebase are features you want there. Forking plugins for larger projects, like add-ons to large frameworks, is especially useful. Unused and unmaintained software is often removed from package repositories without notice and one day your project just won't build anymore. This is a terrible situation to find yourself in and when you do, it's often too late. The source code is already gone. Forking more volatile or unmaintained libraries can help prevent this problem.

In other cases, the software may be hard to read, or poorly documented. In those cases it's best to adopt these projects if they're small or confined to a narrow problem-set. It's not a good idea to pin large parts of your software to unreadable or poorly documented frameworks, but the risk can be tolerable for these small, single-purpose libraries and extensions. Forking the project and adding your own documentation can be useful in some cases (and contributing back is usually welcome), but often it's best to just add notes in your own code that explain any nuance or complex behavior. You may also be able to improve the experience of using an unintuitive library by creating a thin wrapper with better conventions and naming.

With these few exceptions in mind, it's best to stay away from projects that don't meet at least the majority of the criteria in this section. Taking on another project's technical debt won't help you ship software faster or guarantee higher quality for your users.

ROLLING YOUR OWN

In some cases it'll be to your advantage to simply build a tool or library yourself, and while that decision can involve substantial risks and often a significant time investment, it's not something to outright avoid. It shouldn't be the first option you should consider, and there are absolutely domains where rolling your own solution is either a good bet or a horrible idea most (if not all) of the time.

Let's look first at when it's preferable to build something yourself, and it may surprise you that the most important justification isn't technical at all, it's business. Secret sauces aren't usually found in Open Source projects; if they were, they'd just be called sauces. If a specific approach, technology, or implementation would give you a business advantage or allow more nuanced integrations with your desired features, then it can be extremely beneficial to write that code yourself. As an example, Pine.blog, a Social Feed Reader and Blogging service I run, has an in-house feed parser. Parsing and extracting information from feeds is critical to a feed reading service and rolling my own was the only way to guarantee that it worked the way Pine.blog's features demand. RSS feeds on the Web are often poorly written, invalid, and error-ridden, and feed parsing libraries often focus on parsing feeds that are well formed and valid (a much easier task). Customizing an existing parser would require a library with hooks, buttons, and levers that just didn't exist, and if it had, Pine.blog would have been bound to its rules, conventions, and preconceived notions of what feed parsing requires. That wasn't acceptable to me, so I built my own. However, like with Pine.blog's custom feed parser, rolling your own solution can result in a massive amount of new work, so it's worth thinking hard and evaluating your options before just assuming that work yourself.

In some cases, you may find it beneficial to implement multiple different parts of your software yourself, and you may not have the time or bandwidth to write them all. Your time is finite. You cannot afford to build everything from scratch. Perhaps taking on one or two custom solutions prevents you from taking on another that's actually more important for your project. In this case, think about which custom solutions benefit your business and productivity the most, not which ones would be the most fun to develop or the most intellectually satisfying to have designed.

PUTTING IT ALL TOGETHER

At this point, we've reached the end of our discussion of starting and managing your business. We've covered a lot, and yet there's a lot that's still missing. Hopefully, you have a better understanding of the kinds of things you need to do before you can start building your software. You should have a basic understanding of how to structure products, how to design your pricing tiers, how to stay motivated, and how to evaluate technologies. Let this discussion ground your thought processes as time goes on. The goal posts in this section are fairly generalizable and adaptable. If used properly they should help you structure and run your business regardless of what products you offer or services you provide, but groundwork is just the beginning. We have two more important discussions ahead of us. So far we've focused on the business side of things. Even when we've discussed technology or features, they've been focused through the lens of how those features and technologies benefit you and your business. We did this because, as developers, we tend to ignore the business side of things. We don't put much stock in the techniques and insights developed by the business communities. This is a mistake and one that can doom your whole endeavor. That said, you can't launch software with just a business plan and a healthy work-life balance. You still need to actually build software, so let's do that.

Exiting the Cave

Let's Design a Thing

So far, we've concerned ourselves with the overall ideas that will govern our thinking while we build the company and its services. Now, we're going to get our feet wet with real software and real designs. To do that, we'll need a service to build. For our purposes in this book, we'll be discussing a service I launched in June 2020 called Nine9s which provides no-fuss uptime monitoring for developers on a budget. First, we'll cover the service, and its target market, costs, and revenue model. Then we'll cover the business goals of the service. And in the following chapters, we'll get into the gritty details by diving into the design, implementation, launch, and marketing. By talking about an actual service, you'll get to see real, practical examples of everything we've talked about in prior chapters. Talking about implementing a service in abstract is often a confusing and pointless exercise. With Nine9s, we can explore how real business decisions factor into building software, analyze the real world costs and revenue model, as well as the cover the implementation of the software. Nine9s is an interesting example, not because it's the most technically challenging nor the most impactful service I've developed, but instead because it's a service that most embodies the lessons I've learned and hope to share with you in this book. In fact, Nine9s was the original inspiration for everything you're reading here. It was in building Nine9s, which took two weeks of full-time work from start to finish, that I became aware of just how much I'd learned about building stable and maintainable software. The implementation may not make the most design-conscious readers happy, and I don't promise that the code is very pretty. Instead, in pulling back the curtain on Nine9s, I promise to shed light on how to actually launch useful, stable, and maintainable commercial software, both quickly and effectively.

ABOUT NINE9S

> I'm super excited to announce the release of Nine9s, a service providing simple, no-fuss uptime monitoring for developers on a budget. Whether you're a hobbyist with a blog, an indie-dev working on some side projects, or a small dev shop, Nine9s is here to make sure your site is up and responsive for your users and to alert you of any slowdowns or outages.
>
> Announcing Nine9s.cloud 🎉, brianschrader.com

Nine9s is an Uptime Monitoring service. Once a user signs up and sets up their website, Nine9s periodically checks their site to see if it's still responding and working well. If Nine9s detects a problem with the site, it sends the site owner an alert via text message and email. Then when the site goes back to normal, Nine9s confirms this by alerting the user again to let them know the issue is resolved. Uptime Monitoring services ensure that site owners can be sure that their site is up and running and that they're alerted when problems occur. It's a fairly simple but powerful service that can detect problems ranging from overall downtime and slowness, to expired TLS/SSL Certificates. Nine9s provides its users with metrics and dashboards for each site, a full REST API, Webhook-based alerts, and a public status page so that site owners can choose to show their users when the site is experiencing an issue. Overall, Nine9s is designed to provide a simple, easy-to-use, but full-featured solution for developers and hobbyists looking for inexpensive Uptime Monitoring. As a bonus, Nine9s is also powered by 92% clean and renewable energy, limiting its environmental impact.

WHY UPTIME MONITORING?

> I've used Uptime Monitoring services for years, but I've always been left slightly dissatisfied. There's lots of great services out there and they do a lot of stuff, but they either feel like overkill, cost way too much, or don't quite do what I need. That's why I built Nine9s.
>
> Announcing Nine9s.cloud 🎉, brianschrader.com

Like I mentioned in the release blog post for the service, Nine9s aims to fill a gap left by other Uptime Monitoring services. Nine9s is explicitly targeted towards independent developers, bloggers, hobbyists, and others who need Uptime Monitoring that's not only super easy-to-use, but also very inexpensive. Larger Uptime Monitoring services like Pingdom (now SolarWinds), UpDown, Uptime.io, and PagerDuty are incredibly full featured solutions for medium to large organizations. In fact, Adventurer's Codex, a company I co-founded, used Pingdom for years to monitor our software. These services are often well-built and offer worldwide monitoring, but they can also be expensive ($100-$180 annually for the lowest tier). This is because they often support more complex features than most small shops require. These services are also often missing features that would be required to address what (to me) are pretty common needs. After doing a bit of market research, I discovered that there aren't many Uptime Monitoring solutions that target the same market I was considering. There seemed to be a gap. That's when I decided to build Nine9s.

Uptime Monitoring is also a fairly simple service to develop. It requires little computational power, minimal data storage, and short, quick user interactions. There's no large quantity of images to store, no video or audio to process, no long running background tasks, and no complex business workflows. Users need to be able to set up and configure a site, view some dashboards, add some contact information, manage their billing information, and manage an API access token. That's basically it. This reality allowed for Nine9s to be built quickly. The use-cases are simple, the service isn't very complex, and once it's up and running it doesn't require much maintenance. In all, it's a great service for a small software firm to build and maintain, and these same factors make it a great candidate for demonstration purposes here. Whether the business decisions behind Nine9s are sound remains to be seen. At the time of writing the service has only been available for less than six months.

THE FEATURES

While, in a nutshell, Nine9s offers Uptime Monitoring, let's look a bit deeper into the exact features: what they do, and their value propositions.

Endpoint Monitoring and Dashboards

At the core of Nine9s is, of course, the ability to monitor sites, or what Nine9s refers to as Endpoints. Endpoints are just

URLs that the user wishes to have Nine9s periodically check. Once activated, Nine9s will start monitoring the given URL to determine whether or not the site is responding with a valid response. Users can see the status of their Endpoints, browse the recent history of each Endpoint's status and response time in an interactive dashboard, as well as configure the different criteria for each Endpoint depending on their needs.

In most Uptime Monitoring services, Endpoints are typically considered to be in one of two states: up or down. This binary distinction is easy to understand, but is often not useful in all cases. Additionally, it's very common for services that are under heavy load, or experiencing networking problems, to respond more slowly than normal. This lag in response time is often missed or ignored by other monitoring solutions. To solve this, Nine9s considers an Endpoint to be in one of three possible states: ok, down, or degraded. If an Endpoint is ok, it has responded within the preferred time window and returned a response that fulfills the user's specified criteria. A down Endpoint either failed to respond within the maximum allowed time window or has an invalid or expired TLS/SSL Certificate (if desired). A degraded Endpoint, on the other hand, can mean a few different things. Users can specify a preferred maximum response time which is different from (and less than) the maximum allowed time used in the down criteria. This number represents the threshold for normal operating behavior. If Nine9s detects that an Endpoint is responding slower than what is preferred, the Endpoint is marked as degraded. Additionally, Endpoints can be considered degraded if the TLS/SSL Certificate is going to expire within 7 days. This option is configurable by the user, but is On by default. Endpoints can also be configured to appear on the user's public status page, and to use either GET or HEAD requests for the periodic checks depending on the user's preference and what their service supports. By default, Endpoints are not made public and use HEAD requests to save the bandwidth and processing power of the service being checked.

Email and SMS Alerts

Users can choose to be alerted when Endpoints change status. Users can request that event alerts be sent to email addresses and (optionally) phone numbers when Endpoints go down, degrade, or recover. These messages include an explanation of what caused the change to occur. This allows users to know about changes to their service as soon as possible so that they can mitigate the possible damages or scale up their services accordingly. The number of alert destinations or Contacts is dependent on the user's subscription tier.

Public Endpoint Status Page

If a user of Nine9s wishes to share the status of their Endpoints with their users (i.e. for diagnostic or public communications purposes) they can enable their Public Status Page. Each Endpoint can be configured to appear on the status page separately, ensuring that only the information that the user wishes to be made public is public. This Public Status Page shows the list of public Endpoints including their name, current status, and recent uptime history.

The status page also includes an RSS feed for each Endpoint so that anyone can follow the updates and changes of the given Endpoint automatically. Each entry in the RSS feed includes information about the status change as well as when Nine9s detected the change. These feeds can be used for internal debugging purposes, public consumption, or even for external services to use in providing more detailed metrics.

Full API and Webhook Alerts

Nine9s also includes a full REST API that allows users to manage their account, configure Endpoints and Contacts, enable and disable the status page, and delete their account entirely. The API allows users to build tools to automatically enable and disable monitoring during system upgrades, or even build internal tooling using the historical data in the API.

Additionally, users can take advantage of Webhook Alerts. These alerts are similar to the SMS and Email alerts above, but instead of sending a text or an email, they send HTTP requests to a given URL. Developers who wish to build tooling to automatically handle changes in the status of their Endpoints can also use the Webhook Alerts to trigger processing on their own systems to restart troubled servers, file JIRA tickets, or kick off other business processes according to their needs.

PRICING MATRIX

Now that we've covered each of the features that Nine9s supports in depth, let's look at the breakdown of each of the pricing tiers and see how they fit our criteria from before.

There are three overall tiers that Nine9s supports: a basic free tier, a mid-range premium tier, and a high-end deluxe tier. Each of these tiers has slightly different features, and each is designed to accomplish a different goal while still providing users with a solution they can use to fit their needs. Each of the tiers fulfills the use-cases for a segment of users, and gives everyone a chance to try out the service before committing to upgrading to a paid tier. This ensures that users always know what they're getting, what they should expect, and generally how the service works before making a financial commitment. Let's look at each of the tiers in detail and explore what goal they're trying to accomplish and how they go about fulfilling the need of a given Customer Segment.

	Standard	Premium	Deluxe
Dashboards	✅	✅	✅
API Access	✅	✅	✅
Webhook Alerts	✖	✅	✅
Public Status Page	✖	✅	✅
Alert Destinations (Email & Text)	✖	2	10
Total Endpoints	2	5	10
Check Frequency	Hourly	5 minutes	1 minute
Monthly Price	Free 🎉	$2	$5

The Nine9s Pricing Matrix

The Free Tier

Nine9s' free tier acts both as its free trial and a complete solution for certain kinds of users. Looking closely at the pricing matrix above, you'll notice that the free tier allows users to monitor two total Endpoints, browse their history, configure their dashboards, and access the API, but not receive alerts when Endpoints degrade or go down. This is for many reasons, some practical, some business-related, and some financial.

From a practical standpoint, there are users who may wish to check their site's recent responsiveness and who could build tooling to poll the API for changes to their Endpoint's status. Providing a service for free with a requirement that a user do some additional work is not uncommon. This tier allows those users, who are perhaps incredibly cost-sensitive, or who want to monitor free or hobby projects to do so at no cost, and while these users don't contribute to the financial stability of the project, their Endpoints take little compute power to monitor (because of the check frequency period). This allows free users to try out the service and possibly even convince other users with more demanding monitoring needs to sign up for the service.

There are also users who may just wish to try out the functionality of Nine9s before committing to a paid upgrade. It's incredibly beneficial for services to offer some sort of free trial for those users wishing to try out a service who (especially on the web and especially as time goes on) are incredibly unwilling to sign-up for anything that forces them to pay up front. Providing some sort of limited functionality is one option, while other services opt to providing access to the entire suite of features but for a limited time. Both approaches have their advantages and disadvantages, but because of my desire to fulfill the hobbyist use-case, I opted for a limited feature (not limited time) free tier.

On a financial front, while sending emails is effectively free, sending SMS messages is decidedly not (although they are fairly cheap). Rather than allow for free users to receive emails, but not texts, I chose to disallow alerts entirely.

The Premium Tier

The primary goal of the Premium Tier is to allow users to configure Email, SMS, and Webhook Alerts for Endpoint status changes. The addition of these features effectively makes Nine9s a competitive and complete Uptime Monitoring solution for anyone needing budget monitoring. This tier also includes the option to enable the Public Status page and therefore better communicate outages with site visitors. The Premium Tier is designed to meet the core needs of anyone in the target audience. Users can monitor a total of five distinct URLs as well as send alerts to two different Contacts (each contact can receive both SMS and email alerts).

Most marketing literature says that when companies offer three paid tiers, the middle one is by far the most popular. When it's three tiers, with one free, the cheapest tier is the more popular of the two paid tiers. Using this information, Nine9s is designed to turn a profit with most paid users opting for the Premium tier rather than the Deluxe tier.

The Deluxe Tier

By design, users don't need to upgrade to the Deluxe tier to get access to additional features — the Premium Tier offers complete access to the entire suite of features Nine9s offers. Instead, while the Basic and Premium tiers differ based on included features, the Premium and Deluxe tiers differ in scale. You just get more. The Deluxe tier allows for double the number of Endpoints to be concurrently checked (ten not five) and a total of ten Contacts can receive alerts when outages or degradations occur. The Deluxe Tier also reduces the check interval to one minute for users who require literally up-to-the-minute knowledge of their site's status. Effectively, this turns the Deluxe Tier into the "Pro" offering we discussed earlier. It is designed for site owners with more than a few sites, or sites that tolerate a lot less downtime than the Premium users.

Notes About Flat Pricing Tiers

Astute readers may notice that there appears to be no limit to the number of emails, Webhook requests, and SMS messages that a given user could receive over a given time period. While sending a lot of HTTP requests (and to a lesser extent, emails) is effectively free, sending lots of SMS messages is not. This means that, since the Nine9s pricing tiers are flat fees, a given user could cost the service more per month than what is made from their monthly fee. The reasoning behind this decision is fairly simple and has two components. First, while SMS messages aren't free, they are still quite cheap. Additionally, the SMS provider in this case, Twilio, has a finite available budget, which would eliminate the risk of drastic overspending. If the monthly budget is exhausted, users would still receive an email alert and the Nine9s admin (me) would receive an alert from Twilio explaining the situation, leaving more than ample time to fix the situation on the backend. Secondly, instead of complicating the pricing even further, flat-rates give users confidence that the price of given service won't balloon and cost them much more than they expected. When you're targeting a price-sensitive audience, this is really important. In the end, siding with simplicity of implementation, and pricing with guardrails in place to prevent over spending, won out over more complex implementation or less transparent pricing.

Architecture by Example

We've discussed the business goals for Nine9s and what features it supports. In this chapter, we're going to inspect the thought process I used when designing the service. We're going to take a look at a few concerns, tradeoffs, and criteria and see how they informed the system design and helped me choose the tools I used to build Nine9s in June of 2020. The sections in this chapter will try to accomplish two primary goals. First, we'll lay out the technical requirements for Nine9s, and then we'll discuss how software can be used to fulfill those requirements and fit our criteria from before. Second, we'll use this opportunity to explore common Web architecture practices. Web application architecture is a topic that's rarely discussed in the community at length and when it is, the conversation tends to center on the specific tools used rather than the overall design and reasoning. Personally, I've had many early projects die because I didn't know how to properly design them. I didn't know what tools existed, nor how to use them to solve my problems. These days, you rarely need to build infrastructure software yourself; there are lots of great, free tools already out there. If you're already familiar with architecting and designing Web applications, then you may find some of this discussion familiar, but you should begin to see how the criteria we discussed in the previous chapters can be applied to real software. To those who aren't familiar with architecting web software, I hope this discussion helps shed some light on the concepts involved and provides you with a starting point for further investigation.

WHAT WE NEED TO DO

Before any design decisions can be made, it's important to first lay out what responsibilities the software has. To do this, take the list of business requirements and map each one to the different types of technical tasks needed to complete it. When constructing this list of responsibilities, don't worry too much about the specifics of each feature or how it will function. At this point, just focus on the range of different things your software needs to do. For Nine9s, consider at the list below:

- Serve a Website
    - Public Pages (home page, support pages, etc)
    - User Registration, Login, Logout
    - Manage Endpoints, Contacts, and other User Data
    - Payment Processing
    - Tier-based limits for user permissions
- Serve API requests
    - Authenticate users
    - Serve user data
- Periodically check Endpoints and record results
- Send Alerts (email, SMS, Webhooks) when Endpoints have issues

Each of the items in the above list are directly pulled from the features and pricing in the previous chapter. Importantly though, this list doesn't include any system-level administration, auditing or reporting. Most developers tack these things on later, but we're going to anticipate them in advance. Here's an additional few things we'll need to implement to ensure our software works and works well.

- Basic System Auditing and Reporting
    - When is the system having issues
    - What are the issues
- System Backups and Restore
- Essential system security and automatic intrusion alerts

With the list of our requirements complete, we can now discuss how we're going to implement them. We're going to start each section with a short overview of the topic at hand and then explore the decisions that lead me to choose the software I did when building Nine9s.

HOSTING

Before we dive into how Nine9s works, we need to set some boundaries so that the decisions behind the design make sense. For both simplicity and cost-saving measures, Nine9s is hosted on traditional Linux Virtual Private Servers (VPSs). VPSs are just rentable virtual servers that live in someone else's data center. Sticking with traditional VPSs, over more modern and fancy solutions, not only gives us the flexibility to architect our system how we want, it also allows us to really dive in and understand what's really going on with our software, how it's functioning, and how to secure and maintain it. Maintaining servers has gone out of vogue in recent years, and some of that is for good reason. Maintaining servers takes time and effort and requires certain knowledge outside of what a typical developer may have. That said, running your own servers allows for a lot more flexibility and portability. Doing so also ensures that you're in control of nearly every aspect of your business. If you are dependent on the flavor du-jour for hosting (i.e. server-less or other trends) it can lock you into a given platform, overcomplicate your application (especially for a small business), and balloon your out-of-pocket costs. There's lots of great resources out there to help you run your own servers, and learning to do so is an extremely useful skill.

Since Nine9s will run Linux, I needed to pick a flavor. Ubuntu is a very common choice, both because of its overall popularity and active development community, and also because of its stable release cycle and adoption of Long-Term Support (LTS) releases. No one ever got fired for choosing Ubuntu.

However, for Nine9s, I chose CentOS: the community edition of Red Hat Linux. CentOS aims to preserve compatibility and security over launching new features, and is generally a more conservative choice than even Ubuntu LTS. That said, CentOS requires a bit more work up front since some common packages just aren't installed by default. This is because CentOS tends to be conservative not only in the timing of new version releases, but in what content is installed in each version as well.

While we won't be diving too deeply into the deployment and configuration side of Nine9s, I do want to take the time and recommend using Docker to manage your services, deploy software, and handle networking. Docker (with Docker-Compose) makes it easy to develop, test, and deploy your software and it also makes it easy to move pieces of the software around if you need to scale your service. Nine9s uses Docker for almost everything because, in my experience over the last several years, Docker makes deploying, upgrading, migrating and managing services really quick and easy. If you're not familiar with Docker and Docker-Compose, that's fine. They're by no means required to launch software, but they are really great tools to have in your toolbox and I highly recommend looking into how they can help you build better software.

THE WEB APPLICATION

With hosting out of the way, the next step was to set up and configure something to answer requests from the Web, to serve the website, answer API calls, and allow users to manage their account. For this Nine9s relies on a traditional Web application design: the code runs behind an Nginx Reverse Proxy that will handle TLS/SSL termination, HTTP/2, load balancing, static asset serving, and gzip compression. Nginx is a popular Web server that's very easy to configure, works with a variety of tools like Certbot for TLS/SSL Certs, and serves as an excellent reverse proxy.

You can optionally use Apache for this purpose, but Apache (while great at serving static files and rendering PHP pages) isn't a great reverse proxy.

The Nine9s database lives on the same server as the rest of our application for simplicity, listens for requests from the web application and answers them accordingly. Since Nine9s doesn't allow users to upload assets like images or video, all data is stored in the database and there's no need for things like Object Storage.

If your service does deal with assets like video, audio, images, or other large files, you should investigate Object Storage solutions like Linode's Object Storage, Backblaze's B2 service, or Amazon's S3. Object Storage is designed to provide storage for large, infrequently updated files like profile images, user photos, etc. There are a multitude of reasons why you shouldn't store these assets on your servers. Large assets take up a lot of disk space and cost a lot of bandwidth to serve, which could drastically inflate your costs. Additionally, if you do need to upscale your service, you will run into issues serving those assets when they're spread across multiple servers. There are lots of tools you can use to add support for Object Storage to your application, and most are very easy to use.

The Nine9s' application is written in Python and uses the Django Web Framework to serve web requests and connect to a database. The Django REST Framework (DRF) plugin for

Django makes it trivially easy to create extremely powerful REST APIs. Django and DRF are both very well-known, stable tools for web developers in the Python community, and I've used them for years. As mentioned in a previous chapter, the Python Web community essentially marches to the beat of Django releases, and that includes DRF. Both are used by large companies and multiple large organizations actively sponsor both projects. Both are long lived, and full featured. Django also provides Long-Term Support (LTS) releases that remain supported for a full three years. Django provides a number of benefits for developers including it's automatic Administrative Backoffice (sometimes called Django's killer feature), its powerful Object-Relational Manager, and its ability to generate automatic database migrations. Each of these features are absolutely essential for Nine9s because they reduce development time, prevent common bugs, and allow us to focus on what really matters. Importantly, because Django is an older style of Web Application Framework (from the pre-SPA era), it also includes a templating engine out of the box, which makes it easy to build powerful webpages quickly and effectively.

DATA STORAGE

When it comes to storing application data, Nine9s uses Postgres as its database server. Postgres is an incredibly feature-rich, free, open source database server that's used by companies both large and small. Unlike a lot of other database servers, Postgres' default settings are much more conservative and tuned to provide a lot more data integrity and consistency. This means that, unlike some other solutions, with Postgres you don't need to do a lot of configuration. It just works. I choose Postgres for a few other reasons though too. Postgres works great with Django and DRF, and Django specifically has lots of additional features that leverage the immense power of Postgres' ever growing feature-set. Additionally, while Postgres is a relational database at its core, it also supports what it calls JSON and JSONB fields in its relational models. This means that Nine9s can also leverage Postgres to provide No-SQL functionality inside our relational database. If needed, Nine9s can get all of the functionality and performance of a traditional relational database, and the flexibility of a No-SQL database in one powerful tool. Last but certainly not least, Postgres' documentation is top-notch. As we've already covered, the community provides documentation on the PostgreSQL dialect of SQL, configuration information, and most importantly, the Postgres official documentation has lots of User Guides that cover, in detail, how to support and maintain production Postgres servers. Like Django, Postgres fit our criteria very well.

APPLICATION CACHING

It's rarely appropriate to worry about performance in the early phases of a project. Most problems can be made "fast enough" for our purposes on the Web. Performance optimizations consume time and resources for usually very little business gain. However, sometimes there are very simple things you can do to improve the performance of your application that take almost no work to develop. While we're not going to focus too much on performance for this discussion, Nine9s does try to take advantage of any easy wins if possible. Adding application-level caching is probably one of the easiest ways to gain some quick performance benefits with little work. It can be tricky to implement, so you need to be careful and not spend too much time on it, But, done well, caching can drastically improve your app's performance. Because Django supports application caching by default, there's actually very little configuration to do.

Django's documentation recommends memcache, a high-performance, key-value caching server originally developed for LiveJournal, so that's what Nine9s uses. If you're looking to reduce the number of overall technologies in your stack, you may choose to instead use Redis, since it's already used in another part of the system (more on that later). While there are plugins for Django that make it possible to use Redis as its app cache (and I have used them in the past for a variety of things) I opted to stick with what's supported by default in Django for this project. The official Django caching support with memcache is robust, feature-rich and widely supported, plus unlike its Redis counterpart, it's fully documented.

There are a number of benefits to using the Redis cache over the memcache solution. However, because of its lack of useful documentation and often unsupported feature-set, adopting it requires diving deep into the source code of the plugin. If your application requires distributed atomic-locks, you would want to use Redis over memcache because of its built-in support for distributed locks. It's common for applications to use memcache for simple app caching, like we'll be doing here, and to use Redis for frequently changing application data and global replication since Redis supports clustering. Both of these use-cases are beyond the scope of this book.

SCHEDULED AND PERIODIC TASKS

Most simple Web applications receive requests from the Web, process them, and return some response. If no requests come in, no processing is done. Nine9s needs more than that. It needs to be able to schedule and perform tasks outside of the request/response cycle. For example, the system needs to periodically check the status of active Endpoints and sending out alerts if changes occur. It would also be useful if it could delegate future work on behalf of a user outside of the request/response cycle in order to defer optional or long running tasks and return results to our users faster. This is where task processing comes into play. Task processing enables us to define certain kinds of discrete work that can be acted on later or work that needs to be done on a schedule, whether periodically or at a scheduled time.

Most languages have a task processing library that glues together a few other tools to provide your application with an environment to accept, queue, delegate, perform, and resolve asynchronous tasks. In most cases these solutions involve five parts, though the names may vary.

1. **The Task Broker:** A piece of software that acts as a queue for what tasks need to be completed. The broker may also handle things like rate limiting, task prioritization, multiple task queues, and dependency tracking.

2. **The Result Store:** This piece stores the results of tasks after they've completed. While technically optional, a Result Store drastically improves the functionality of your task processing and allows for much more complex and powerful workflows.

3. **The Task Processing Library:** Usually, this library provides a convenient API for the developer to use in order to control, monitor, schedule, and delegate tasks to the other parts of the system. This library may also provide a convenient way to consume tasks from the Task Broker queues and return results to the Result Store.

4. **The Scheduler:** This software handles the scheduling of certain tasks. If you're familiar with Linux's cron utility, it's similar to that, but it often allows for much more sophisticated operations.

5. **The Task Worker(s):** The workers are the part of this whole stack that actually perform the actions. Your application could have one or many workers that are actively waiting for new tasks working them, storing their results, and waiting again.

For those new to this kind of paradigm, it may seem overwhelming, but don't worry. While it can be daunting to set up the first time, once you do master this toolset, all kinds of doors open to you. Your applications can defer expensive work which speeds up your website for your users, you're able to perform more complicated workflows, and it becomes possible to build entirely new classes of applications.

Only one of these pieces, the Worker, contains any custom code. The rest of the functionality is provided by other tooling. There are lots of great tools for task processing in each language and environment, but since Nine9s is written in Python, it was easiest to stick with Python for task processing. It's important to remember though, you don't always have to be so consistent. If for example, your worker needs to perform intense mathematical calculations, a high-level language like Python may not be ideal. Instead, you may opt for something like Go, Rust, or Swift. Because of the distributed nature of this kind of task processing, as long as your worker can communicate with your broker and backend, you can use whatever tooling you want. That said, Nine9s uses the following tools for task processing.

1. **Task Broker**: RabbitMQ
2. **Result Store**: Redis
3. **Task Processing Library, Scheduler, Worker**: Celery

For the Task Broker, Nine9s uses RabbitMQ. RabbitMQ is an open source, industry standard message broker that excels at providing fast, feature rich queueing, and cluster management tools. It also supports clustering if your application requires multiple distributed brokers. In short, RabbitMQ will grow with your business no matter how big it becomes.

For our Result Store, I opted for Redis: a fast and powerful key-value database. This means that unlike a relational database, Redis only stores things in two columns: a key (a name), and a value (the thing you want to store). Redis is industry standard for this purpose and in every situation I've used it for, it has worked well. It operates in-memory making it super fast. One downside to this speed however, is that Redis doesn't persist its data by default. This means that if your server was ever reboot-ed or if it crashed, you would lose everything. That said, Redis does support persisting its data to disk to prevent this outcome, it's just not enabled by default.

One nice additional benefit of using Redis is that we can also leverage it to provide cache storage for user data. While Nine9s doesn't use Redis for this purpose, Pine.blog uses a simple version of Twitter's timeline fanout system to construct user timelines and this system uses Redis as a backing-store as well as using Redis as a task result store as described in this section.[11]

Celery is a great tool to have in your Python developer tool-box. It's extremely flexible, powerful, and feature-rich. Celery also integrates very nicely with Django Web Applications, making it a perfect fit for our stack.[12] Admittedly, it can be challenging to configure the first time, but once you understand it the possibilities are endless. Celery has been a staple of the Python community for years and has wide support for a number of different Task Broker and Result Stores if our choices here don't fit your needs. Celery has been critiqued for not being suitable for very large or very decentralized clusters of workers. While this may be true at the massively large scale of a company like Salesforce, Facebook, or Instagram, Celery has been well suited for every use-case I've thrown at it; from long-running, distributed, scientific computing to large-scale RSS feed parsing, so I knew it would be more than enough for Nine9s.

While Celery supports a variety of different Task Brokers and Result Stores, the documentation recommends both RabbitMQ and Redis for those roles, which is yet another reason to choose them as your preferred solutions. However, this recommendation is not always valid. I've built and designed services that use Redis for both of these roles and systems that don't implement a Result Backend at all. One benefit of using Celery is that it's flexible enough to meet a variety of needs.

SENDING ALERTS

Once the periodic tasks find an issue and record it, Nine9s needs some way to alert the user that their Endpoint's status has changed. The feature matrix says that the system needs to support three different kinds of alerts: Email, SMS, and Webhooks. Since Webhooks are just HTTP POST requests and it can send those on its own. This means that Nine9s just needs a way to send both email and text messages. For both of these solutions,

I opted to use a third-party provider. The code will determine when to send a message and what message to send, then after that it will contact one (or both) of these services and let them handle getting the message to the recipient.

Because of the easy to use API and straightforward billing, I opted to use Twilio as the text messaging provider. Nine9s was my first commercial project that needed to integrate text messaging and I found that Twilio was a great fit.

As for emails, here we're going to stay pretty vague. There are lots of email providers out there: focused providers like Fastmail, providers that may come packaged with your domain like Hover.com, and (of course) there are the big providers like Gmail, Office365, and others. Because of the beauty and openness of Email as a standard, we only need an email address, password, and an SMTP server to send email, and each of these providers grant easy access to that information. Some providers, like Fastmail, allow you to create email address specific passwords for programatic use. Similar to API keys, these tokens keep your real email password secure and allow you to configure additional permissions to protect how those credentials are used. If your provider does allow you to use App Specific Credentials, it is highly recommended that you do so.

PAYMENT PROCESSING

Like Nine9s, your software will be a commercial endeavor, it will need some software or service to accept payments, take care of invoicing, charge customers, provide refunds, handle disputes, and manage recurring subscriptions. Most sites just outsource this work to a payment processor. That said, it's common for developers to assume that you can build the product and then tack on a payment solution after the fact. I know, I fell into this trap myself. While you certainly can do that, it's much easier to integrate your payment solution as you go. Handling money is incredibly complex and subscriptions are even more so. Aside from supporting typical edge-cases like customers disputing charges and changing credit card numbers, payment processors also handle supporting multiple payment providers, providing automatic currency exchange, and allowing you to customize subscription pro-rating. Integrating a payment processor into your application is a big task, and one that can be stressful. After all, that code literally powers everything on which your business depends. Get it wrong and you may not get paid, or you may anger your customers and drive them away. Payment processing is a lot of work, but it doesn't have to be scary.

Nine9s uses Stripe to handle payment processing. I've used Stripe for years and it has incredibly good documentation, powerful dashboards, and a complete test sandbox that makes understanding, integrating, and (crucially) testing code easy. Stripe also offers a wide variety of payment options to customers, and minimizes the amount of data you need to store on your own database. It's important to note that there are legal requirements to handling payments, but Stripe deals with most of those details. Their documentation describes how your service needs to behave to comply with the legal requirements and guides you through the whole process. Personally, I'd recommend reviewing Stripe's documentation early in the product development cycle because there are crucial business decisions you'll need to make when handling payments. A lot of these scenarios are uncommon and easily missed when you haven't developed a commercial product before. Stripe does a great job of laying out all of the possible scenarios your systems will need to account for no matter whether you are integrating one-time purchases or subscriptions. Actually doing the integration work is pretty straightforward, once you understand the concepts and process involved, and Stripe's testing system makes it easy to confirm that your system works as expected.

DISASTER RECOVERY

Most developers don't think about disaster recovery until it's too late. Don't be one of those poor souls wishing they'd backed up their databases or that they'd tested the restore process before it was needed. There are multitudes of horror stories about companies, even large ones, that have some minor problem that explodes into a huge issue because of a failed restore or lack of reliable backups. Instead of being admitted into their illustrious ranks, we're going to discuss a quick set of best practices that ensure that not only are you making regular backups, but that your are testing your data restoration process regularly to ensure it works as expected.

While the details of the implementation will be left as an exercise for the reader, the gist of the implementation will be as follows. Every 24 hours, generate a full backup of your database. This can be a simple cron job that simply dumps your database, through gzip, to a file on disk.[13] This process is incredibly simple, and takes minutes to build and test. Backing up your database is easy. Ensuring that those backups are actually useful is another thing entirely.

Test restoring your database regularly. Ideally this process should be done automatically, but a set of calendar reminders can suffice for a time. Restoring a database is fairly simple, and of course, it should always work.[14] But the word "should" has doomed more programmers than perhaps any other single term. If something "should" work, then it probably doesn't. I've found that easiest way to ensure that your database backups are actually useful is use them directly for reporting. For a multitude of reasons, you don't want to do ad-hoc reporting on your production system. Complex reports are often taxing and involve sorting through lots of historical data. This can drastically degrade the performance of your production systems. Most competent businesses perform their reporting on a separate reporting database. This gives us an opportunity. If, after your nightly backup is created, you restore that backup to a reporting database, then you'll know the restore process works. Better yet, you'll know that it keeps working. If, at any time, your reports aren't up to date, that means that either your backup or restore process is broken. This manual check works great because it ties the business need of daily reporting to the technical need to backup your data and routinely test your restore process.[15] That way, if you ever do need to perform a backup and restore of our database, you not only know that it will work, but the script to do so will have already been written and tested.

AUDITING AND REPORTING

Now that your data is backed up and can be restored to a reporting database, you'll need to consider what kind of reporting you'll actually want to do and whether you have the data in your data model to answer the questions you might have about your business. For our purposes, 'auditing' simply means that our system is capturing and recording when and how things fail. Auditing can be done in a number of ways, and which way you choose depends on the design of the system and how much time you want to devote to complex reporting. Lots of developers don't implement any sort of auditing or reporting, and therefore they're completely oblivious to how their system is serving their users. Whether you opt for a full featured reporting solution, or you build something from scratch, isn't really relevant. As long as the auditing captures the information necessary to answer your questions, then it's working fine.

For our purposes, 'reporting' simply means that you can use the data captured by your auditing systems to provide answers to your questions. Reporting can be done in a number of ways from manual ad-hoc queries, to admin summary pages, to implementing a full reporting solution.[16] There's a number of great approaches to reporting, and what you choose will largely depend on how easily and quickly you want your questions answered.

Nine9s uses a slightly convoluted reporting system, but it's one that I've used multiple times in a lot of my apps. Every few hours, Celery pushes an administrative reporting task onto the queue. This task runs in a separate queue and it has top priority so it's not blocked by other long-running tasks. It checks the current length of all of the system queues and validates that everything is running properly, then if it detects an issue, it uses Django's email module to send an alert email to Pushover which forwards the message as a push notification to my phone.[17] Nine9s also runs a job at midnight UTC-time that counts the number of new users and new paying subscribers and sends me a similar notification. I have a similar system set up for Pine.blog and d20.photos. This system is pretty simple, but it works well and it's easy to implement and tweak. I then occasionally test the system restore process manually to ensure my backups work properly.

Adventurer's Codex, on the other hand, has a full suite of reporting dashboards, alerts, and charts that are powered by Redash. The reporting database, just like we discussed in the above, is fed from the latest system backups. This ensures that our backup/restore process works and allows us to perform ad-hoc reporting without burdening the production system. I highly recommend Redash, which can be easily self-hosted using Docker, if your application grows and gains a sizable user-base. I've been using Redash for years and it's only gotten better and better.

Regardless of how you audit and perform reporting, it's important to gain insights into how your business is doing. Some of this work is overkill at the beginning, especially if you have very few users, but over time you'll want to establish a robust and dependable reporting system that can quickly give you some understanding of how much revenue you make, where users get confused, how many users continue to use your service once signing up and for how long, and what features are the most used and valuable to your user-base. This insight helps you build better software. Without this information, you're flying blind; with it, you're able to better steer your business and improve the experience for your users and the profit for you.

SYSTEM SECURITY

Like with system auditing, you can't just install or configure a prebuilt security library and call it a day. There are a lot of tools you can use to improve the day-to-day security of our systems. These tools can be used to check for potential vulnerabilities in your software's dependencies, conduct intrusion detection on your servers, and encourage plain good practice when setting up, installing, and configuring Web applications. Security can be a tough topic to discuss because there's no fool-proof way to do it. Every system can be hacked. Designing a secure system doesn't mean being invulnerable, instead it means taking into account the security risks of each of your decisions, minimizing the attack vectors that someone could exploit, and (critically) minimizing the harm that could be done if you are attacked. That last factor is incredibly important. For example, it's long been industry practice to not store user passwords directly, and instead store a hash, which is not easily reversible, and then compare the user's credentials to that hash. This prevents an intruder from gaining access to the actual text of the user's password for potential use against other services, and also minimizes other attack vectors. Deciding how to store (or not store) critical data is important. There are a number of simple things you can do that will drastically improve the security of your application. Documentation can also be a huge help. Most big tools and services have figured out the best practices for developers using their software. All you have to do is find that guidance, and implement it. Linode's guide, "How to Secure Your Server," is probably the best starting point if you're trying to shore up the security of your virtual servers.[18] For their parts, Django and Postgres also have guides and instructions in their documentation that guide you through security best practices.[19] [20]

HONORABLE MENTION: BASH

When building software, it's often tempting to overcomplicate things. Whether you over design a system, over abstract a core component, or over complicate your implementation with high-minded concepts, you're essentially just making your life more difficult later on. Before you try to build anything, consider if it can be done with just a bash script. Often times complex tooling can be replaced with relatively simple scripts, run by cron or some other utility. One of the beauties of working with actual VPSs is that you can script and automate basically anything. You're not limited to what can occur within a request/response cycle, you're not limited to shared compute limits or other constraints inherent in managed solutions, and you're free to tweak, script, and customize basically everything. Need zero-downtime deploys? Bash can help you. Need a routine backup or restore process? Bash can help you. Do you need to send emails to yourself when things appear in a log somewhere? Bash can do that. Do you need to have some custom script run before your app server boots to ensure some state or files are in the right place? Bash is your hero. So many modern computing tools are just fancy replacements for things Bash or other shell languages have done for decades, and they're often slower and more complex, than the script equivalent. Granted they're probably more readable, but they're rarely as dependable. In all my time hosting, managing, and deploying software, bash scripting is the best tool I've found. I use it to do basic reporting, handle my deploys, script preflight checks, manage backups, handle admin alerts, control system behavior, and so much more.[21]

If you aren't familiar with bash as a programming or automation tool, then I urge you to dive in. The language is pretty ugly, and the syntax can be incredibly archaic, but you will not find a more useful tool. With small operations like yours, you rarely have time to devote months to learning fancy deployment tech, set up industry leading but cumbersome solutions, or automate things in the most modern way, but you often don't need to. You just need your software to work and work well. Developers are often either afraid of or dismissive of bash as a tool. Granted, if you're using Windows, such a tool is essentially useless, but I won't comment on using Windows as a development platform. On Linux, and to an extent on macOS, there is no better option. Use bash. It's old, it's crufty, and it's exactly what you need.

HONORABLE MENTION: TURBOLINKS

Nine9s doesn't have a modern dynamic frontend. It's an old-style website, rendered on the server and sent to the client as essentially static HTML. This conveys a huge number of benefits, primarily in matters of time investment and development simplicity. But old-style interfaces are fairly limited in a number of ways, after all that's why modern front-end solutions exist.

Turbolinks is a library from Basecamp, the company behind, well, Basecamp and the email service Hey. Like Nine9s, Hey and Basecamp are largely rendered server-side and contain little Javascript and no frameworks, like React or Angular, though you could be forgiven for not noticing, because Turbolinks enhances their site and makes it feel modern and streamlined. Turbolinks is a drop in library that requires very little customization.

> Get the performance benefits of a single-page application without the added complexity of a client-side JavaScript framework. Use HTML to render your views on the server side and link to pages as usual. When you follow a link, Turbolinks automatically fetches the page, swaps in its <body>, and merges its <head>, all without incurring the cost of a full page load.
>
> Turbolinks Documentation

In most cases you can simply include the Turbolinks Javascript library at the bottom of your base template and be done. This library is a fantastic example of how simple tools and clever tricks can save you weeks or months of development while still providing your users with a great experience. Perhaps a full and complete single-page app would be slightly better, but Turbolinks can easily get you 80% of the benefits with almost no work at all. Admittedly, Nine9s doesn't actually use Turbolinks, at time of writing, but I've used it for d20.photos and I'm incredibly excited to add it to my standard set of tools.

PUTTING IT ALL TOGETHER

If you've gotten this far and are concerned about the volume of work that lies ahead, fear not. A lot of the designs, techniques, and approaches discussed in this chapter are very simple to implement, often with just a few short lines of code, and most of this is just industry standard practice that many of you are probably already doing without knowing it. Like we discussed in the introduction of this chapter, system architecture is not often discussed in developer or business focused contexts. The purpose of this discussion has not been to scare you, but to clarify the technical and business decisions behind different aspects of the architecture. In thinking about your system from this perspective, you're laying the foundations for a possible future, while also not requiring yourself to actually implement that future now. Your job is to make sure that when the time comes, you can expand if needed; not to scale your software now. Your approach should be to let your tools do most of the work, leverage what already exists, and ensure that your software is stable, secure, performant, and cost-effective.

Instead of focusing purely on the technical merits of a given solution, think about how those solutions impact your productivity as a Developer, your future feature-set as a Product designer, and your costs and potential revenue as Business owner. Above all, the aim of designing a system architecture, and of choosing technologies to implement it, is to ensure business success. To succeed, the business must be flexible, grow, improve, launch features, and be free of huge mounds of technical debt. Implementing new features and improvements shouldn't require rewrites. In fact, you should try to avoid rewrites at almost any cost, and you can only do that if you make the right choices up front. That doesn't mean you should agonize over your technology choices. You can apply the criteria in previous chapters to the design laid out in this one. If you are still not sure, just go with the technology or technologies recommended by the tools you're using, and be skeptical about adding more tools once you've started building. That said, you're going to make mistakes, especially at the beginning. If you find that your architecture or your tooling doesn't account for some facet of your business, or your technology choices don't quite fit the need you have, that's fine. It will happen. What's important is that you recognize those problems and shortcomings early, learn from them, and recover.

ARCHITECTURE REVIEW

Having discussed both the architecture of Nine9s and the tools were used to build it, let's take a step back and review the design. How does it accomplish the business goals we discussed before? What shortcuts were taken? What are the limiting factors of the design and how can they be addressed if needed? Where is the cruft going to build up?

What We Do Well?

From what we've laid out, the design of Nine9s prioritizes the ability for new features to be developed quickly and easily because it uses powerful and standard tooling. The design leverages big, robust frameworks, a stable and dependable operating system, and industry-standard tooling. The design allows for flexible, asynchronous workflows and typical request/response processing. There is a basic auditing and reporting framework so that when failures occur, they can be handled. The design also ensures that the system can be improved and expanded if necessary. All it would take is a little bit of time and effort to add lots of modern accessories or drastically upscale if that's the goal. In short, the software can grow alongside the business and it requires minimal work to maintain.

What Got Cut?

The design of Nine9s doesn't take advantage of a lot of cool and powerful modern tech. There's no dynamic front-end, no large-scale custom tooling, and no WebSockets. While each of those could be added later, this also means that for now, the interface design will be pretty basic and the infrastructure probably won't make the front page of Hacker News. What's especially limiting is the lack of a secret sauce. Without any special, custom tooling, Nine9s is limited to what features and perks already exist in big frameworks. There's nothing stopping another company from using the same tools and recreating the service, and in fact there's nothing stopping you from using this information (especially the information in the next chapter) to do the same. In practice this isn't a concern, but it does mean that Nine9s will always be a bit behind the latest trends, always following a slow, and stable path.

Where's the Cruft?

There's a saying in parts of the software development community that you can never completely get rid of cruft. You can reduce it, sure; but after a certain point, all you can do is move it around and spread it out. Cruft comes in many forms. It can be generated by partial refactors, unfinished design changes, left-over bad designs that were never updated, or even un-migrated legacy data. Some people, myself included, call this Technical Debt (an apt metaphor). Like monetary debt, Technical Debt carries interest that makes it harder to pay down over time. The longer you wait to pay down the debt the bigger it gets and the harder it is to pay off. All projects have cruft, or debt, and some try to manage it through refactors and other pay-down schemes, but it's impossible to eliminate all of it. Experienced developers can often look at a design and intuitively know where the cruft is likely to build up. Developing this intuition is difficult, but once you do, it can be very helpful. Start by looking at your design. Consider what parts are essentially fixed in size and scope once built out, and what parts grow? The build-up of cruft is mostly a by-product of how often a given section of code is changed. The less often you modify your code, the less cruft can build up. This is because cruft emerges as a direct result of code being written, changed, and deleted. Cruft is not a natural phenomenon that builds up over time like stalactites forming from dripping water in a cave. Cruft forms because you create it, though often unintentionally.

In the Nine9s design discussed here, the biggest source of cruft is probably in the view-layer. This is very common. The worker nodes that perform the actual checks, are very simple and don't need to be changed much. The monitoring, auditing, and reporting is similar as well. The data model, as you'll see later on, is simple but it's also full-featured. It shouldn't need to grow much beyond its initial state. Only the view-layer (and the API that it's tied to) will change frequently enough to accumulate significant cruft. Once you take the time to investigate your software and develop your intuitions about where the cruft will most likely accumulate, you can take steps to minimize it.

Time To Start Building

Now that we've discussed system design, the Nine9s tech stack, and reviewed its pros and cons, it's time to dive into the process of actually building software. While there's still a lot more business related matters to cover, we're going to shift into development mode for a bit and come back to those things when they're more relevant to our progress towards eventual launch.

Useful Patterns & Questions

So far we've discussed how to design software systems. Now it is finally time to dive into the actual process of developing software. While this next section won't be a complete step-by-step tutorial, we will discuss interesting approaches and clever tricks that improve your productivity and help ensure your software is stable and feature-rich. Remember, your goal is to provide useful functionality to your users that is easy to understand and use, and we'll discuss how you can write robust code that you can easily maintain and improve over time. Here we will explore a few useful development techniques and discuss how you can use them to build powerful and stable software. To help us along and provide practical examples, we're going to look at how Nine9s models a user's Endpoints, and how that model is designed to be minimal yet feature rich and performant. Then we're going to see how you can leverage the power of an otherwise archaic academic concept, finite state machines and state transitions, to help you write cleaner, more concise, bug-free code. This journey may seem a bit off-topic at times since it has little to do with the business concerns we've discussed thus far. However, the techniques described in this section have helped me build and maintain robust and powerful software that requires minimal maintenance and support. As I've said before, refactors and other redesigns are incredibly unproductive, and the best way to avoid refactors is to not need them. In my time building software, I've developed and gathered techniques from all corners of the software world. Some ideas are my own, but most are taken from blog posts, books, talks, and conversations with members of the community. A good business plan is necessary for a successful business, but so is good software. Up until now, we've focused on how to develop your business, now let's dive into how you can improve your software development skills and actually build the software your business will sell to its users.

BUILDING DATA MODELS

Throughout this section we're going to use the data model Nine9s to illustrate various concepts. In this section, we're going to investigate how you can improve your data model and your application's overall performance and auditability by asking yourself the right questions. Before we can dive into the questions, we need a data model to examine.

In this section we're going to discuss two core concepts from the Nine9s data model: Endpoints and Checks. Endpoints model the URL that a user wishes to monitor. Endpoints are "checked" periodically and those results are recorded in a Check. Once an Endpoint is checked, its state and other values updated to reflect the status we observed. If an Endpoint transitions to a new state, alerts are sent to the user. Additionally, a user is able to activate and deactivate an Endpoint in situations where they'd prefer to temporarily stop monitoring and receiving alerts. This allows users to schedule downtime. Consider the following fields for the Endpoint model.

- `name`: A human-readable name

- `endpoint_url`: The URL to monitor

- `user`: A user that owns the Endpoint

- `status`: A status that can be either active or inactive

We also discussed, in earlier chapters, that we'd like to offer the user the option of performing checks using either a HEAD or GET HTTP request. To do this we'll need to capture this preference from the user. Additionally, we'll need to add a field to capture whether or not the user wishes to add a given Endpoint to their public status page. This adds the following two fields to our model.

- `check_type`: A value that specifies whether to perform GET or HEAD requests when checking an Endpoint.

- `public`: A boolean value as to whether or not the Endpoint is shown publicly.

Once an Endpoint has been checked, we need to ensure it passes some criteria. Beyond ensuring that it responded at all, we want to allow the user to specify if an Endpoint should respond with a valid TLS/SSL Certificate and set a value for the maximum preferred response delay for their Endpoint to be considered healthy. This adds two more fields to our model.

- `ensure_valid_cert`: A boolean value that records whether we should ensure that the Endpoint responds with a valid and un-expired certificate.

- `degradation_threshold`: An integer value representing the maximum number of milliseconds the given Endpoint should take to respond before being considered degraded.

This concludes the discussion of the majority of the fields needed for our Endpoint model. There are a few others we will need before our model is ready to be finalized, but the need for those will become clearer after a discussion of our Check model.

For our purposes, a Check is a record of whenever an Endpoint is, well, checked. The results of each Endpoint inspection is recorded in a Check record. A Check corresponds to one and only one Endpoint, and an Endpoint has multiple Checks containing the history of the Endpoint's status over time. Checks therefore record the Endpoint it corresponds to, when the check occurred or began, and how long the check took to complete, in order to compare it to the degradation threshold for the Endpoint and graph the results over time. Checks also capture whether the Endpoint failed any of the custom criteria set by the user, in our case this means capturing whether the Endpoint responded using a valid TLS/SSL certificate. Finally, the Check captures the overall state of the Endpoint after the check was performed: whether the Endpoint is considered ok, degraded or down, along with any message or error report. The Check model contains the following fields:

- **endpoint**: The Endpoint that the Check corresponds to.

- **checked_at**: The time that the check occurred.

- **response_time**: The amount of time, in milliseconds, that the Endpoint took to respond to our request.

- **failed_cert_check**: A boolean value recording whether the Endpoint responded with an invalid certificate if it was required to do so.

- **status**: The overall status of the check.

- **message**: A textual message to share with the user about the current status of the Endpoint.

These fields contain the majority of the data needed to alert the user when issues occur, but astute readers may notice an oversight. Even with the combination of both the values contained within an Endpoint and its associated Checks, with these fields alone, it would be difficult for Nine9s to construct queries to answer even basic questions in a performance-conscious way. Let's look at a few example questions and see how the data model described above falls short in answering them. Then let's turn to how this model was improved to better answer such questions.

Asking the Right Questions

Using the Nine9s data model above, let's consider a few practical, real-world questions to see how the model could answer them. When you perform the same exercise with your own software, be sure to stick to questions you know will be asked by either yourself as an administrator or your users. In asking these questions, you're looking to see how your data model solves the real-world problems it is likely to encounter, how well it performs, and what shortcomings exist. Only after that's done can you start to craft solutions to those problems.

First, let's consider a seemingly trivial question: What's the current status of a given Endpoint? In order to answer this using the above data model, Nine9s would need to look up the most recent Check for the given Endpoint, since the Check contains the data about an Endpoint's status at the time the check was performed. To find that Check, Nine9s would need to find all Checks associated with the given Endpoint, sort them by their checked_at timestamp (or primary key since it's an auto-incrementing integer) and then return the most recent value. With a small number of Checks in the database, this wouldn't be much of an issue, and even with a somewhat large dataset indexing could help reduce any bottlenecks, but fundamentally, the same core problem exists: as more Checks are recorded, and more users sign up for the service, the software must sort through more historical data. This slows down the system as more users sign up. This is a pretty classic problem with Web software and especially with historical data. To remedy this problem Nine9s includes the most recent Check's data on the Endpoint itself and ensures that, when Checks are recorded, both copies of the data are updated simultaneously. By adding the following fields to the Endpoint model, Nine9s can answer our question by simply querying for the given Endpoint, and inspecting its current status directly without querying for the historical data at all. This eliminates any potential for slowdown because at no point did the database sort through an ever-increasing amount of data. Here's the full list of fields that were added to the Endpoint model in Nine9s to address this concern:

- `last_check_status`: The status value from the most recent check that was performed on our Endpoint.

- `last_check_message`: The message (if any) that describes any abnormal behavior during the last check performed on our Endpoint.

- `last_check_at`: The time that the last check on our Endpoint was performed.

Now, some experienced developers are probably looking at this solution with concern. As many developers know, storing the same data in two places is often just setting yourself up for data inconsistencies. If a Check were ever to be successfully recorded, but the values on the Endpoint failed to update, the data would be inconsistent and invalid. This is an important insight. I've been bitten many times by this same concern and generally I prefer to recalculate or derive values rather than store potentially inconsistent data in multiple places. Don't worry though. In this case, Nine9s uses the power of transitions and atomic operations (more on that in the next section) to ensure that the data is always duplicated correctly and rolled back completely if an error occurs.

Next, let's ask another question. When did an Endpoint change states? That is, when did the Endpoint go down or recover? This question is fairly obvious and is definitely something a user would want to know as it's one of the core functions of Nine9s as a service. Given the Endpoint in question, Nine9s would need to fetch the list of all recent Checks for that Endpoint and compare the status of each Check to the one proceeding it. If the statuses aren't the same, then the latest check in that comparison recorded a point where the Endpoint changed states. At this point, the software would need to check and see if the Check transitioned the Endpoint to the state being asked for. All of this searching and filtering is expensive, and, just like before, it gets more and more time consuming when large numbers of Checks need to be filtered and sorted. Once again, indexing could help, but at the end of the day, the code would still need to search and compare each Check to the proceeding one. Instead of doing this, Nine9s records another additional data point on Check model that gets populated when the Check is created. This field simply contains a boolean value denoting whether or not the given Check caused the Endpoint to change its status. You may think that, in order to calculate this value, Nine9s would need to perform a query to fetch the most recent previous Check to compare to, but since the Endpoint model already has the result of the last check, because of the fields we discussed earlier, the values can simply be compared to those prior results when creating a new Check. In this way, Nine9s never needs to query the Endpoint's history and doesn't need to constantly re-optimize and re-index its database. Consider this addition to the Check model:

- `did_change_status`: Whether or not the given check caused a change in the Endpoint's overall status.

This value can simply be indexed to aid in find all of the Checks that caused an Endpoint to change its status historically. In that case the software can query for all Checks on a given Endpoint that contain the status of `down` and a `did_change_status` value of true. Simple, easy, and efficient.

THINKING IN STATES AND TRANSITIONS

With any non-trivial data model in any real application, there exists the possibility for data, especially redundant data, to get out of sync and ruin the data integrity of the system. This problem becomes especially common when data moves through complex or long-running workflows. In some cases, preserving your application's data integrity can be easy. Simply minimizing the sheer amount of data your application collects can drastically reduce the surface area on which these problems can occur. That said, real-world applications often need to cache or copy data to multiple places, utilize shared data in a distributed manner, or process entries using complex workflows that can be stopped, started, and reversed by the user at any time. It's common for developers to implement their workflow systems without considering or protecting against these kinds of complex use-cases. For example, if your application includes a photo upload pipeline where images need to be uploaded by the user, asynchronously compressed and resized, then distributed across the world to multiple edge nodes, then each of these steps can (and will) fail in real-world use. How your application handles that failure and either recovers or reverts back to a previously known safe state will have a huge impact on how challenging and cognitively burdensome your software is to maintain and improve. In our example, your application may succeed in uploading the user's image to your servers but fail, for some reason, at resizing the image to one of the three sizes your system requires. In this case, your application may simply try processing the images again, but you'll need to consider what you want to happen to the other two images that were resized successfully. Do you decide to throw them away and properly clean up your image database? Do you forget to clean them up and cause large numbers of unused images to balloon your storage costs? Or do you attempt to detect which images succeeded and only retry resizing the image that failed? Each of these approaches have upsides and downsides and it can be tricky to handle each of these cases properly. To better handle these kinds of situations, it's useful to reduce the surface area where these problems can occur. But how can you reduce the possibility of problems when you can't reduce the amount of data or simplify the workflow any further?

Finite, explicit states and state transitions are words common enough in software development to have considerable cognitive baggage associated with them. For those who've studied classical Computer Science, which I did not, you may be reminded of Finite State Machines and other theoretical computing terminology. While Finite State Machines are incredibly useful, and there are a number of great libraries and technologies that can be used to add FSM functionality to your applications, this isn't exactly the concept we're going to be discussing. Instead, we are going to take certain basic elements and ideas from FSM theory and apply them in our software in order to create a set of boundaries and pipelines through which our application's data can flow. We're going to use FSM to help us wrangle the data we collect and streamline how it's processed so that we can more easily discover, debug, and fix potential problems.

Before we dive into a practical example, let's wade into the murky swamp of words and grab hold of a few key terms that will serve as our foundation for the rest of our discussion. First, we have states. Most of you will probably be familiar with this term. A state is the description of a system or grouping with any discernible set of values present at a given time. Your application has a state (running, starting, off, etc.), and your individual data records have a state. These states always exist, whether we name them or not. A system or grouping of data can have any number of possible states, depending on how we define them. Our job is to limit the number of states as much as possible. We couldn't minimize or reduce the amount of data, so now we try to reduce the amount of possible states. We do this by creating constraints on our data and on how it transitions from state to state.

For Nine9s, an Endpoint can be in three possible states: active, inactive, or unknown. In the Active state, our application is checking the health of the Endpoint URL and recording results. In the Inactive state, the Endpoint may have a history but is not undergoing any active monitoring. In the Unknown state, the Endpoint has just been created but has no history and has not yet been persisted to the database, so no health checks can occur. In the Unknown state, an Endpoint may not even have a name or URL, but it must have both to be in either the Active or Inactive states. Defining these states and what values must or must not be present when certain data enters each state is critical. These constraints limit how defensive we need to be when checking values for `null` and they provide us with a certain set of guarantees when dealing with a certain record. By enforcing these states we lower the total amount of cognitive load when analyzing a section of code, and we can also ensure that our application can easily detect invalid data or invalid states and flag them, or better yet, avoid them entirely and always revert to a known, defined state when things go wrong. In software development, we depend on implicit states all the time. We may enforce a policy that a field cannot be `null` in our database, or that a value must be universally unique, or that a foreign key actually correspond to an existing value in another table. We just don't often think of these as states, instead we think of them as constraints on a single value or set of values. Thinking explicitly about these states can help you better design and grapple with complex flows in your application, but how does data move from one state to another?

Transitions manage the way data flows from one state to another. Transitions are what we call the defined process by which data can move into another state. For example, the Endpoint model can only move from the Unknown state to the Active or Inactive states if it has both a name and an Endpoint URL. State transitions, whether implicit in the form of database constraints, or explicit in the case of literal transition functions or methods, govern how data is manipulated. By being explicit and defining functions or methods in your code that transition a given record or records from one state to another, if and only if those records fulfill the criteria to transition, and always using those explicit transitions to move data around, you reduce the total surface area on which issues can occur. Let's look at a simple example. Nine9s needs to check to see if a given Endpoint is healthy and record the results accordingly. To do this, it needs to make a request to the Endpoint URL, validate some criteria, and then update the state of the Endpoint and record the Check data. Here we're going to ignore a lot of the error handling and extra processing that the production code contains for the sake of simplicity. Consider this naive implementation of an Endpoint check process:

```
def check_endpoint(endpoint):
    response = requests.get(endpoint.endpoint_url)

    if endpoint.is_valid(response):
        endpoint.last_check_status = 'ok'
        endpoint.last_check_at = now()
    else:
        endpoint.last_check_status = 'down'
        endpoint.last_check_at = now()
        endpoint.last_check_message = 'Endpoint is down'

    endpoint.save()

    Check.objects.create(
        endpoint=endpoint,
        status=endpoint.last_check_status,
        checked_at=now(),
    )
```

This, rather simple, example may seem correct. Admittedly, it ignores many of the data points in the actual data model for simplicity, but even with these few data points there are a number of important potential problems. First off, you may notice that if an Endpoint were ever to go down, and then recover, the last_check_message would not be cleared. This would pollute the data model with old, invalid data. Secondly, the check_endpoint function doesn't ensure that a Check record and updated Endpoint values are both persisted together. If the Check fails to save, the Endpoint could still be persisted, causing data integrity issues. Thirdly, because the state change is implemented implicitly (by just setting a bunch of independent values), whenever the application would need to update an Endpoint's state elsewhere in the code, that implicit transition would need to be re-implemented, or worse copied and pasted. Manually, independently, and implicitly transitioning states causes a huge number of bugs. One section of code may reset the last check message when transitioning, where another may not. This leads to bugs that are confusing and difficult to debug, and fixing issues with this behavior often relies on accurate, technical descriptions of the the issue from users, something both rare and difficult to obtain.

Let's look at how these issues can be addressed simply and easily. First, ask yourself: what does it mean for an Endpoint to "go down" or "recover"? What is involved in that process. Instead of simply saying that an Endpoint "can be down", consider: How does it go down? Each line of code in a transition is one step in a process. With this frame of reference, you can see that state transitions are rarely instantaneous. Though certainly possible, rarely does the state of a complex collection of data only rely on a single value to change during a transition. In those cases it's probably fine to simply set `object.state = 'closed'` because the `state` property is the only value that changes when the state of the object changes. For an Endpoint, this isn't the case, there are a whole range of fields that need updating when it transitions between states. Let's take a look at what the Endpoint check method from before would look like if it instead used simple `go_down` and `recover` transition methods.

```
def check_endpoint(endpoint):
    response = requests.get(endpoint.endpoint_url)

    if endpoint.is_valid(response):
        endpoint.recover(response)
    else:
        endpoint.go_down(response)
```

In this example, the transitions implicitly save the Endpoint, and since "going down" and "recovering" don't require a certain initial state there's no further preconditions to satisfy before attempting to transition. Not only is this code cleaner, but it contains a specific set of actions that other code in the application can use when it needs to transition an Endpoint. In this example, the creation of the associated Check record has been moved into the state transition methods and, while it is not shown here, the transition methods are atomic operations. This is because creating the Check is part of what it means to "go down" and "recover". Any change in the state of our Endpoint should be logged for historical analysis by the user. In this example an Endpoint that does not respond but fails to log that fact will not complete the transition to the down state.

Crucially, transition methods like those in the example above should always result in an Endpoint that exists in a valid state and clean up bad data if possible. If, during the transition, the Endpoint is not able to fully move to its new state, the transition should abort and revert the data back to the previous state as completely as possible. This lessens the potential for side-effects from failed transitions and guarantees that after an Endpoint is told to recover its state will be ok in all cases where that transition succeeds. State transitions should be among the most stringent and codified sections of your codebase. The number of guarantees your transitions are able to make to the rest of your system is inversely proportional to how much cruft builds up wherever these transitions are used. Put another way, the more you can guarantee about how your data will look post-transition, the fewer bugs your code will have wherever you perform that transition.

Let's briefly discuss one of the lesser explored, but incredibly important tricks in that last example. The astute reader may have noticed, and certain developers may have wrinkled their nose at, what may seem to be a grave oversight in the example: What happens when an Endpoint that is already in a down state is told to go down. Conversely, how can an Endpoint that's currently ok possibly recover? And what would it be recovering from? The answer is both incredibly powerful and potentially dangerous if used incorrectly, so let's explore it in a bit of detail. Academically speaking, a system can be thought of as transitioning between states every single time a data value changes. Every toggle of a switch, every renaming of a folder, everything is a state transition. Sometimes, those transitions cause the system to move from a given state back to that same state. Text editors are a good example of this. When a document is open and ready to be used, the text editing program is in a state of "Awaiting Data". In this state, it blinks the cursor and waits for the user to type text. Whenever the user starts typing, the text editor can be thought of as moving from the "Awaiting Data" state, into the "Rendering" state where it enters the typed text into the current document, and then transitioning back to the original "Awaiting Data" state. From the user's perspective, text is being entered in a document. The UI of the text editor isn't changing or flashing between screens with each keystroke, but in a way, the editor is moving through this transition each time a key is pressed. For our purposes, the text editor's "Rendering" is more of a transition than a distinct state. In that way, the editor moves from "Awaiting Data" to "Awaiting Data" seamlessly. The beginning and end states here aren't actually important. What's important is the transition. Moving from a given state to the same state may have an important meaning in your application, or it could be a no-op. You could choose to define that the ok state can only move to the down state and vice-versa, but we can also define the ok state as being able to transition to itself. The transition then ceases to be just a method of moving from one state to a different state, and instead more conveniently contains the business-process by which that Endpoint performs its duties. Transitions are the process by which your application data changes. They are the allowable actions your system can take to perform the business need, not just the programatic process of setting some values on a record.

By thinking of your data model, and your application at large, in terms of a discrete set of finite states and the transitions between them, and codifying those transitions in explicit, dedicated sections of your code, you're fundamentally reducing the surface area for bugs and improving the readability and maintainability of your codebase. If a user were to experience an issue that occurs when an Endpoint recovers, you know exactly where to look, since there's only one place where that recovery process is specified. When used in this way, data model states become guarantees you make to yourself, a promise that when an Endpoint is active it will always have a name and a URL. These guarantees make it easier to reason about complex software and manage the consequences of migrations and large changes. Transitions codify your business process in one distinct location in your codebase. They ensure that the data going through the transition must be in a certain state when the transition begins, and will be in a certain state when it ends. They ensure that failures are accounted for, and that they are handled properly. Perhaps most importantly however, state transitions force you to reckon with the true complexities of your system. They require you to give each state a name and to account for how each state can transition to the next. Explicitly considering each possible state, and how each state can or cannot transition to another, will surface potential issues sooner and shed light on potentially unseen problems early in the development process. Giving a name to each state and each transition forces you to think about what each transition actually does and what each state actually means. Naming things is hard, but it's also illuminating. By using states and state transitions, you're using the the act of naming to help you prevent problems in the future. What's in a name? I'd argue: everything.

> For magic consists in this, the true naming of a thing.
>
> Ursula K. LeGuin, A Wizard of Earthsea

PRICING TIERS AS STATES

Now that we've discussed simple data models and state transitions, we are ready to discuss how these concepts can be used to simplify and shore up normally complex operations. Specifically, we are going to consider how these concepts can be applied to implementing a payment system. Nine9s already uses these concepts in this way, so throughout the discussion, we will use Nine9s as an example. I've implemented payment systems and subscriptions in my software in a number of different ways over the years, and this was, by far, the most simple, expressive, and powerful paradigm I've found to wrangle the problem of payments and tiers.

As we discussed earlier, Nine9s supports three subscription tiers: standard, premium, and deluxe, and in Nine9s, a user has a tier property that contains the value of the subscription tier they're in.

```
class Tier:
    standard = 'standard'
    premium = 'premium'
    deluxe = 'deluxe'
```

This tier property is essentially a kind of state that the user is in. In fact, Nine9s be uses the concept of states and transitions to move a user between subscription tiers when they upgrade or downgrade. Since a user can only be in one tier at once, this model fits really nicely.

Nine9s also uses the Tier model, which in the example above has three string properties, is the home base for all business-level product constraints and logic. Essentially, this class contains the code-level representation of the feature matrix from our earlier discussion. By putting everything in one place, the tiers are not only easy to adjust and mock for testing, but this centralization improves the overall readability and clarity of the code. Whenever a section of code needs to know what a given limit is for a resource or action, Nine9s can ask the Tier model. We're not going to cover all of the various constraints and code for each limit here, but what follows should give you a framing for this idea.

As we laid out in our discussion about the different subscription tiers, each tier has different limits and features. Recall that each tier has a different Check Interval (i.e. the amount of time between checks for a given Endpoint). Tiers also allow users to have a different maximum number of Endpoints or Contacts, and paid tiers allow users to activate their Public Status page or add Webhooks. If you structure your tiers like this, you'll want to include these constraints as must as possible in your Tier model to improve consistency. Let's look at an example:

```python
class Tier:

    @classmethod
    def check_interval_for(cls, tier):
        if tier == cls.deluxe:
            return timedelta(minutes=1)
        elif tier == cls.premium:
            return timedelta(minutes=5)
        else:
            return timedelta(hours=1)

    @classmethod
    def can_enable_status_page(cls, tier):
        return tier in (cls.premium, cls.deluxe)
```

As you can see, each of these class methods encode one of the values in the feature matrix. The software can refer to these limits anywhere by passing in the User's tier value like so:

```python
if Tier.can_enable_status_page(user.tier):
    enable_status_page()
```

While this is convenient, Nine9s also includes custom properties on the User model to make this syntax even more concise and clear.

```
class User(BaseModel, AbstractUser):

    @property
    def can_enable_status_page(self):
        return self.Tier.can_enable_status_page(self.tier)
```

Once implemented, these methods allow the software to easily verify whether a given user can utilize a given feature, as you can see in the example below.

```
if user.can_enable_status_page:
    enable_status_page()

# OR

if user.endpoints_remaining:
    user.create_endpoint(data)
```

These constraints and limits will automatically adjust whenever the core values in the Tier model are changed. The code becomes easier to read and (importantly) it has a single source of truth for each business-level limit. This makes it easy to tweak or change the limits when needed later in the product lifecycle. It may not seem like a common decision, but businesses change their products all the time, either because they need to compete with other businesses, or because of changes in technology or pricing from third-party vendors. You don't want to be stuck spending lots of time upgrading and modifying different aspects of your code simply because you want to loosen the limits on a given tier. By centralizing this information, you make it so that changes to the tier limits are quick and easy giving you more time to improve your service and make your customers happy.

Subscription Transitions

Let's talk subscriptions. Specifically, let's talk about how a user moves from one subscription tier to another, how that transition affects the user's data, and how your software can manage each of these transitions and limits in a sane, sensible way. Like we mentioned earlier, Nine9s treats the user's subscription tier as a state the user can be in. A user can be in one and only one tier state at a given time and they can transition between tier states by upgrading and downgrading their account subscription. For this discussion, we're going to ignore the payment processing phase of the process. Once your software goes live, a user won't begin the process of transitioning states until after the payment process is complete anyway. For now we're going to assume that a user can freely choose which state to be in and can move between them at will.

First, consider a set of transitions that move the user between subscription tier states. Remember, a user can be in one of three subscription tiers: standard, premium, and deluxe and in effect, a user can go from any subscription tier to any other. A user's default tier is standard which is the free tier. This means that Nine9s has three different transitions. Each of these transitions handles migrating all of the user's data to fit within the bounds of each tier. Importantly, transitions are bi-directional. A user can upgrade from standard to premium but they can also downgrade to premium from the deluxe tier.

Let's look at an example subscription transition, and discuss the key takeaways:

```
class User(BaseModel, AbstractUser):

    @transaction.atomic
    def to_premium(self):
        logger.info(
            f'Promoting user: {self} to premium tier.'
        )
        self.tier = self.Tier.premium
        deactivate_excess_endpoints(self)
        remove_excess_contacts(self)
        self.save()
```

Like it says, this transition handles moving a user from any state to the premium state. First off, the transition is contained within an atomic database transaction to prevent any errors from leaving the user in a corrupted state. Then, the transition logs some information so that the administrators can tell what the system is trying to do, and to which user. The tier property is updated to the correct value, and then various actions are performed. Depending on your business, these actions will differ. For Nine9s, I made the business decision that if a user has more Endpoints than the allowed number for their subscription tier, those Endpoints shouldn't be deleted because the user may still need the historical data. Instead those Endpoints are deactivated so that they're not collecting any new data, and the user isn't allowed to re-activate them or make any changes to them. Though they are allowed to delete it. I also made the decision to delete any excess Contact records the user may have if they've added more than the allowable limit for the given tier. Contacts are not only simple to add and remove, but they also carry no historical data, so deleting them doesn't remove usable user data. Notice that, if a user was attempting to upgrade from the standard tier to premium those two functions would effectively do nothing. Standard users can't add enough Endpoints or Contacts to be targeted by these limits. These methods only act on users downgrading from other higher tiers. This allowed me to collapse both directions into one transition. Also, using Nine9s as an example, keep in mind that a user can upgrade to the `deluxe` tier, add Endpoints, downgrade to `standard` which would deactivate but not remove their extraneous Endpoints, and then they can upgrade to a `premium` subscription. This would trigger the `deactivate_excess_endpoints` call to trigger because the user would have more than the allowed number of Endpoints, but would simply deactivate already inactive Endpoints. No matter how the user gets to this tier, and no matter what path they took, the transition logic holds. Now that we've covered how you can use transitions and states to construct a tiered system, the other two transition methods are left as an exercise for the reader.

USING TRANSITIONS TO WRITE BETTER CODE

Both of the techniques described in this chapter have suited me well. As a developer, it's important that you improve your development skills while building your business. Part of being an indie developer is constantly striving to do better and to do more with less. These techniques, while certainly useful to all developers, are especially useful when you have limited time and need to ship quality software, if for no other reason than because they centralize where problems can occur which can make debugging easier.

Once you've written your software though, you need to make it available to the public. This means hosting your software in a production capacity. A lot of developers are put off by such things, but as we will see in the coming chapter, finding a hosting provider, moving your software to production, and learning to manage servers is just another thing that indie devs need to be able to do. Your software won't make your business success-ful if it's just running on your laptop or stuck in a repo on Github. It needs to be up, running, secure, and available, so let's do just that.

Hosting

Once your software is built and working well, it's time to make it available to the world. If your software isn't running on the Web (i.e. you're distributing an app through an app store) then you won't need to worry about hosting, and you can move on to the next chapter.

Web developers of all stripes are often afraid of or uncomfortable with administering servers. These days, a myriad of tools and platforms exist to help developers cope with this fear. They handle deployment and hosting for you, and in doing so they hide the complexity and increase the cost of running your business. We're not going to use a lot of this modern tooling largely because it's not strictly necessary for our scale and because our goal will be to overcome, not hide, any discomfort you may have with running servers. Fear not though, in this chapter we'll discuss the pros and cons of different hosting strategies and hosting providers. Setting up servers and hosting software is often not as complicated as it is made out to be. Especially at the scale we are operating at, the industry's darling tools are often overkill.

Like many developers and system administrators, I learned to manage servers by doing. In college I wanted to build a website, so I found a shared-hosting provider and did so. Over time, I wanted my site to do more than my provider would allow, so eventually I had to bite the bullet, rent a virtual server, deploy my website on it, and figure out how to manage it. That was many years ago, and while I highly recommend the experience, you probably don't want to delay the release of your software for two-to-three years so you can learn how to manage servers by constantly screwing them up, as I did. As such, like with the implementation section previously, we're going to dive into the processes, procedures, and thought processes that I use when comparing hosting providers and setting up production servers for small to medium sized projects. In doing so I hope to dispel the myths and mystery surrounding hosting Web software and give you the confidence that you too can take control and launch your own software without the need of expensive tools and complicated pipelines. These methods and techniques are optimized to provide low cost hosting, quick deployments, and stable releases, all while maintaining a low cognitive burden. They're certainly not guaranteed to be optimal for large teams or big companies, though they're probably good enough for them too.

CHOOSING THE RIGHT PROVIDER

These days there are a plethora of great hosting options available to developers and businesses on the Web. Whether you need an easy to manage system like Heroku, the full power and flexibility of AWS, simple and customizable virtual private servers, or even bare metal hosting, there are companies large and small that can fit your needs. With so many options and most of them being incredibly affordable, if you know what you're doing, the deciding factor when choosing a hosting provider isn't the quality or quantity of the core service, but rather the ecosystem, tooling, and resources that each provider supports and provides.

Amazon Web Services are well known for their flexibility, manageability, and scalability. Their documentation is pretty good, they offer a complete suite of services to fit basically any need, and lots of great tools exist that integrate easily with their platform. That said, AWS is pretty expensive and many of those costs aren't visible until it's too late. AWS also provides a wide array of tools no matter what needs you may have, but conversely they also push you towards integrating with their proprietary tools and solutions. Personally, I don't feel that the tradeoffs that come with using AWS are worth the benefits for most independent developers largely because of the unpredictable pricing, and proprietary lock-in. This isn't to say that you shouldn't use AWS. That's your decision and you may value those tradeoffs differently. Like with all tools and all services, AWS is certainly a good choice for some businesses, but it's definitely not the best choice for every business.

Traditional Virtual Private Server (VPS) hosting providers like Linode and Digital Ocean are an incredibly attractive option for small and medium sized businesses and are especially useful to start-ups or others with limited funds and tight budgets. Their flat pricing leads to predictable and dependable monthly bills, something AWS simply can't provide. Both Linode and Digital Ocean have great documentation and both support a wide-range of tools and development styles.

This discussion may remind you of an earlier conversation about technical considerations when choosing your tools. This isn't an accident. Your hosting provider is but another tool in your toolbox.

Linode, in particular, offers a range of inexpensive options for companies of all sizes, but their tiers are especially valuable for those on a tight budget. Plans start at $5 per month for a 1 CPU, 1 GB RAM server, which is pretty awesome for beginners. Their other small and medium sized plans are similarly inexpensive. For years, Adventurer's Codex served over 5,000 users every month with two small virtual servers at a total cost of $30 per month for the production environment, and even that was a little overkill. Linode also provides excellent documentation. Their help site offers how-to guides and helpful tips and tricks for managing production servers. So much of running servers is figuring out what needs to be done; actually doing the work is usually pretty easy. Linode's guides let you in on the what and why of running servers and then walk you through the how. Personally, I can't speak for Digital Ocean because I haven't used them as a hosting provider before, but their documentation is also very good. That said, we're going to continue on with Linode for the rest of this chapter. We'll be leveraging their guides and documentation through much of the rest of our discussion, we'll be using their terminology during, and and we'll be using their pricing to estimate our costs.

Full disclosure: I've been using Linode for over 6 years, and Adventurer's Codex, Pine.blog, Nine9s, and d20.photos are hosted on Linode. I've used AWS and Azure before and they're definitely cool and useful, but for my purposes, Linode has always been the best fit.

ENVIRONMENTAL CONCERNS

Let's talk about economics and climate change for a bit. I know this probably isn't the most prescient topic on your mind at the moment, but hopefully I can convince you that it should be. Climate Change is perhaps the single most threatening issue on humanity's radar, and it's entirely driven by the amount of greenhouse gases in our atmosphere. Transitioning to a net-zero or zero emissions future is an enormous undertaking and according to the international scientific community, we have until 2050 to get on the right path. Now, what does this have to do with your software business? Well, software runs on computers. Computers run on electricity, and that electricity is generated using a number of different methods. As a business, whenever you choose to use a new tool, embrace a new platform, or adopt a new paradigm, you're making changes to what is effectively your supply chain. In software, we don't often think about supply chains and supply chain management. Since we're not building, assembling, printing, or shipping physical products we don't need to stop and think about the people who do that work. That said, we do have supply chains, they're just digital. We make choices that impact the world around us. The frameworks, tools, and platforms you choose to use make a statement about your values. They also say a lot about your priorities and they can act as a differentiator for customers.

The tech world is full of stories detailing the awful conditions workers across the world face when they're tasked with building products for consumers. Companies in Apple's manufacturing supply chain have been sharply criticized for employing dangerous practices and being forced to install nets to prevent workers from committing suicide.[22] Fashion companies are often culprits here too. How many times have we heard of clothing being sewn by child laborers.[23] These are the results of bad supply chain management. In software, our supply chains are virtual, but that doesn't mean they can't cause just as much harm.

What follows here is purely speculative and my own prognosis for what is yet to come.

In the coming years, as Climate Change becomes ever increasingly important and solutions ever more prevalent, companies that don't actively choose to participate in the solution are part of the problem, even small companies on the Web. Even though Web traffic, according to estimates, constitutes only a small percentage of global emissions, it's still important to work to reduce that footprint. And it's important that we as developers and business owners contribute to the solutions we as a society face rather than worsen the problems. Whats more, customers will increasingly notice and want to support businesses that are expressly working to reduce their Climate Change impact. Even ignoring the existential threat factor, this is an incredible marketing opportunity for you and your business. If you can show that you're doing what you can to help the environment, certain customers will see that and support you all the more.

The good news is that hosting your business in a way that helps lessen the Web's carbon footprint is actually pretty easy. You can do a lot if you simply host your servers in a data center that relies on clean energy. This might sound intimidating to do, but actually lots of providers are moving towards clean energy hosting already. All you need to do is leverage those providers over others. AWS and Microsoft Azure have already made their commitments to reach clean energy goals, though in my opinion their progress is not inspiring. That said, smaller providers are often able to offer more radical options first. Linode, for example, doesn't run their data centers. They rely on existing data center partners, and some of these already have ambitious clean energy goals. Linode's partner in Europe, Equinix, has already committed to powering their data centers on 100% renewable energy in the coming years and they've already achieved 92% clean energy reliance.[24] In this example, helping to save the planet is as easy as choosing to host your server in London or Frankfurt instead of in Newark or Dallas. That's it. Depending on where you are, you may see longer ping times, but most users won't even notice and you'll be able to confidently state to your customers that your software is powered by 92% clean and renewable energy. When the choice is so small, and the impact so large, it should be an easy choice to make.[25]

CHOOSING THE RIGHT CONFIGURATION

Choosing the size and configuration of your servers can be tricky, but luckily it's pretty easy to change later on if your needs change. The needs of your software will drastically affect the configuration of your servers. Pine.blog and Nine9s are really clear-cut examples of this. Because Pine.blog, by its nature needs to perform a lot of CPU-bound and IO-bound computation (feed parsing, timeline construction, task monitoring, etc) the system is spread amongst multiple, disparate servers. The application and database, along with a small local worker and the task scheduler, live on the main server. This server is significantly larger than the others as it performs a variety of tasks and needs to be able to serve large loads of incoming traffic at a moment's notice. The feed parsing and timeline constructing workers, on the other hand, run on a multiple of much smaller, single-core servers. These servers only do two things: feed parsing and timeline construction. Feed parsing is the far more demanding of the two and is primarily CPU-bound. This means that the only way to improve the performance of the feed parsing system is to increase the core count. On Linode's platform, VPS core counts and memory increase together and bigger servers are more expensive. In this case, it's actually substantially cheaper to leverage multiple 1-core servers than it would be to run one server with the same number of cores. Pine.blog also includes a dedicated task broker and caching server that handles overseeing everything. All in all, Pine.blog, which must parse and reprise over 10,000 feeds an hour, uses one Web and database server, one task broker and caching server, and four worker servers for a grand total of six servers.

Recall that unlike Pine.blog, Nine9s doesn't have intensive CPU requirements. It does have a moderate IO-bound task footprint, but IO-bound tasks, especially network IO-bound tasks, are significantly easier to parallelize. Because of this, Nine9s runs on one 2-core, 4GB RAM server. That means that Nine9s' Web server is half the size of the Pine.blog Web server. Even with this smaller server, Nine9s is able to handle hundreds of outgoing checks per minute, and because of the pricing model of Nine9s, if the service were ever to require more Endpoint checking throughput, the service would make more than enough revenue to pay for this increase in computing power.

As you can see, the configuration your service will require is dependent on the nature of the service itself. In my experience, most simple systems, like Nine9s, can be launched on a 2-core instance, but that may change if your application stores lots of data on-disk or uses significant background processing resources. Opinions about the proper base configuration of web services differ greatly. Some developers like to plan far into the future and anticipate their needs in advance. This can be helpful if the service gets to that point, but can also increase costs significantly and complicate the software at launch which could prevent a timely release or hamper any post-launch maintenance. Marco Arment, creator of the Overcast podcast app and

Tumblr co-founder has put together an incredibly helpful guide for small-business owners and developers looking for server configuration advice.[26] Personally, I've found his guide to be a little overkill for most projects, but even his most powerful and expensive recommended setup is pretty cheap by modern hosting standards.

> Want a scalable setup? Make three ($60/month) [instances]. Two are your webservers and one is your database. Put a virtual load balancer in front of the two webservers ($20/month). At any time, you can then easily take either of the webservers down for a few minutes to upgrade to a higher-powered instance without taking the whole service down. If you get an influx of traffic one day, just clone a few more webservers behind the load balancer. After the load subsides, delete the ones you don't need anymore.
>
> Web Hosting For App Developers, Marco Arment

As developers, we're lucky. Our start-up costs are significantly smaller than that of other businesses with similar reach. A lot of other businesses require tens of thousands of dollars in initial spending and thousands of dollars a month to pay rent and utilities. As Web developers, our businesses can be run for a few hundred dollars in incorporation fees and less than a hundred dollars per month in hosting.

SETTING UP YOUR PRODUCTION SERVER

Once you have a configuration and you've created a server or servers to use as your production environment, it's time to set them up and get your software running. Depending on the tooling you use and the deployment tech you chose, this process will vary wildly. Setting up servers is tough the first time you do

it, but it gets easier as you become less and less afraid or para-
noid about the process. Regardless of how you choose to set up
your servers, there are tons of resources out there to help you.
Linode and Digital Ocean, like I mentioned, have lots of great
guides, but good sample code from other popular projects is
great too. If your service uses Linux VPSs but not Docker, you
might want to investigate the Digital Ocean guide, "How to set
up Django with Postgres, Nginx, and Gunicorn on Ubuntu".[27]
If you followed the guidance in the previous chapters and are
instead using a stack similar to Nine9s, then you should refer to
a few resources and sample scripts I've made available to help
you manage and deploy software. These scripts are published as
Gists on Github.[28] [29]

Once you have your server configured, you should consider
encrypting the disk or the swap files. This is a pretty straightforward process, though it can be confusing the first time. Linode has an excellent guide to help you through that process.[30]
Of course, you should first refer to the ever-important and constantly referenced, "How to Secure Your Server", guide to get
started before doing any further security enhancements.

Whenever you set up servers, there's always a gotcha involved. The process is usually straightforward, but eventually
something will trip you up and waste your time. For me, that
issue was reliably the same thing every single time: Nginx can't
reverse proxy to a local server if the default SELinux security
policy is in place, so I always need to remember to remove that
restriction.[31]

DEPLOYING YOUR SOFTWARE

Once you do get your server up and running, it's time to configure your deploy process. Deploying and updating software on

servers is a task that both happens frequently enough to be important to streamline, and also rarely enough that you might forget the precise set of manual steps you need to take in order to deploy your software. When deploying or updating remember, checklists are key. Checklists are the ultimate sysadmin tool. Whenever you deploy your software, use the checklist. If the process changes, update the checklist. It's been said that checklists are the that reason the military doesn't invade the wrong country. They ensure pilots inspect their aircraft before takeoff, and they ensure that doctors amputate the correct leg. Checklists are your friend.

Aside from constructing a deployment checklist, the second most important thing you can do to ensure your releases and upgrades go smoothly is to remove as many steps as possible and automate the rest. It's difficult to mess up a one-command deployment process. It's much easier to mess up a process with multiple inter-dependent and time-sensitive steps. Over the years I've managed to tune my services to be incredibly easy to upgrade. For example, since Nine9s is written in Python and uses Docker, a deploy is simply a git pull and docker-compose up. Nowadays, even those steps are automated by a bash script. Having such a simple process means that I can deploy quickly, and it lessens the cognitive burden associated with upgrading a service, even when that service has gone without changes for months. If you find yourself struggling to remember what steps to take when deploying your service, or if you make a mistake, it's worth it to try and automate those steps so that you'll never have that same problem again.

LIVING IN PRODUCTION

There are two phases to the software lifecycle: development and maintenance. Once your software has moved onto a production environment and has real data flowing through it, you've moved to the second phase. You may still be launching features and improving things, but fundamentally, things are different now. Any data model changes must be migrate-able, any features must be backwards compatible, any legacy functionality or data must be carried along for the ride. Living in production can be challenging, especially for developers who spend their time mostly working on the initial phase of a project. Massive refactors and rewrites are even harder now and the lives (and finances) of real people are affected by your decisions. Being successful in this phase requires a shift in perspective. No longer are you solely concerned with launch. Now your decisions need to account for the distant future, the users you already have, and the foundations you've already laid. The robustness of your earlier decisions will be laid bare for you. Only after your software is released (even for beta) do the true consequences of your decisions become apparent, and you will most likely have made decisions that you no longer agree with. This is par for the course. However, now that you've entered the second phase, you can't simply dump and rebuild parts of your software that you don't like. In this phase, everything is a migration.

While our discussion thus far has introduced a few tidbits of information and advice that should provide some guidance as you work through the process of building your software, I trust that you already know how to do the majority of that work. Hopefully this section has introduced a few useful coding concepts and dispelled some myths around hosting. Now that you know how to make better technical decisions, choose hosting providers, and design systems, it's time to turn back to the business-side of things. Just because your service is listening for HTTP connections at an IP address on the Internet doesn't mean you've successfully launched anything. At that point, you've simply turned your software on. You've flipped a switch. Launching requires much more than that.

Wrapping Up & Showing the World

Marketing and SEO

As you move out of the development and deployment phases of your project into preparing for launch, you'll need to start thinking about how you're going to market and sell your wares. You may have heard the maxim "build it and they will come", but in my experience such tactics are incredibly ineffective and rarely result in anything resembling success on the Web. Marketing is key. At its core, marketing the process that helps people discover your company and what products and services you offer. Marketing is the hook that pulls people in; the neon sign that entices passers-by. Marketing on the Web is a strange beast, and it takes many forms. Most times, when people think of Web marketing they think of ads: those ever-present, annoying, interrupting, and infuriating banners, popups, and sponsored links that not only crowd out legitimate content, but scoop up and track everything we do on the Web these days. But marketing is far more than just ads and most of it is harmless good practice.

In this section, we're going to dive into how to sell your product. How to show off to potential buyers and drive traffic to your site through good, old-fashioned means. We'll discuss different approaches to communicating about your products, the pros and cons of each, and then we'll dive into the principles of Content Marketing and Search Engine Optimization. For completeness, we'll also explore the seedier world of Web advertising and try to glean what this industry offers us, and if it is worth the price we pay. As you can probably tell, I'm no fan of Web advertising. That said, I have used it extensively in a few projects. In this section I'll describe what's worked for me and what hasn't, and let you in on lessons that took me years of time and hundreds of dollars to learn. Good marketing is really hard to do well, and bad marketing is easy and expensive, but ultimately ineffective. Let's now explore what it takes to get closer to the former, and how to completely avoid the latter.

DESIGNING A LANDING PAGE

Your site's landing page is the first chance you have at convincing potential users to sign up for your software, and there are a lot of ways you can optimize your landing page to inform and convince new users. Every company and every landing page is different, and approaches and styles that work in one domain or business might not work in another. How you design your landing page is up to you and is largely dependent on the values you want to convey; the specifics of the design aren't important in this discussion. Instead, we're going to focus on the goals, function, and features of a good landing page and leave the details up to you. Let's briefly look at a few landing pages from the Web and from software I've worked on, and compare the designs and discuss the reasoning behind those design choices.

A good landing page should give the user all of the information they should need to make a decision before signing up for your service. This advice may sound simple and obvious, but it's really not. If you take a look at the landing pages for popular sites on the Web, you'll notice that some provide essentially no information at all. Twitter's landing page, for example, has almost no content. A grand total of five short sentences, each no longer than eight words is all you get. Modeling your own landing page after Twitter's may seem cool and stylish, but Twitter's landing page exists for people who already know what Twitter is; people who just want to sign up or log in. They've already been convinced to join Twitter. In your case, you need to first convince potential users to sign up for your service. Let's take a look at Twitter's landing page before they were popular and compare it with their landing page today to see how their approach has changed.

Twitter's landing page in 2008 vs. in 2020

As you can see, Twitter's landing page in 2008 gave users a lot more information about what Twitter is and why they would choose to use it. In 2008, the site had a small FAQ on the front page, a video explaining what the service was and a sign up page. Compare that with today's landing page, and the paltry three bullets on the right that tell you essentially nothing. Twitter today has a lot more functionality than it did in 2008, so their marketing pitch has obviously broadened to encompass all that they do. This, in turn, means that the pitch must be more general and abstract. Twitter can do this because, these days, they no longer need to explain who they are or convince users

who go to their site to sign up. Twitter is a major social platform. Their home page doesn't need to market the service, it
just needs log in and sign up options to be useful.

You are not Twitter; your landing page doesn't operate in the
same world as Twitter's does. Your business is much more like
Twitter back in 2008, and since that's the case, your landing
page should explain what your software does, why people
should use it, and what they get out of it. Crucially, if your service requires a paid subscription, your landing page should
strive even harder to convey the value that your service provides. Twitter was, and is, free to use, so convincing users to
spend money was never part of the pitch the landing page
needed to make. To understand this, let's look at an example of
a landing page for a paid subscription service: Pine.blog.

Pine.blog's landing page

As you can see, this landing page is pretty wordy, but it does lay out the main features of the service clearly, and invites the user to either sign up or learn more. The content above-the-fold (i.e. visible before scrolling) also features screenshots of the iOS app. However, while the Pine.blog app is a major component of the service, some have criticized the site for featuring the app so prominently, creating the illusion that Pine.blog is only available on iOS, which isn't actually the case.

Remember to add a prominent call-to-action on your landing page. In the Pine.blog example above, the call-to-action invites users to sign up, whereas Twitter's call-to-action assumes that the person already has an account and invites them to sign in. Your call-to-action should be both prominent and straight-forward. If you're selling a product, your call-to-action would be directing users to purchase the product. If your service offers tiers, like Nine9s, then you'll want to communicate the differences between the tiers clearly and effectively.

▨ Straight-forward pricing

Uptime monitoring shouldn't cost an arm and a leg. Nine9s is designed to be sensitive to your budget. Whether you're a blogger, or a small business we've got the plan for you.

	Standard	Premium	Deluxe
Dashboards	✓	✓	✓
API Access	✓	✓	✓
Webhook Alerts	✗	✓	✓
Public Status Page	✗	✓	✓
Alert Destinations (Email & Text)	✗	2	10
Total Endpoints	2	5	10
Check Frequency	Hourly	5 minutes	1 minute
Monthly Price	Free 🏃	$2	$5

Nine9s Subscription Tier Comparison Chart

The landing page for Nine9s explores the differences between the subscription tiers using a simple grid. This simple presentation gives potential customers the ability to quickly understand the features that each tier provides and it allows them to easily grasp the distinctions As we mentioned in our earlier pricing tier discussion, it might be beneficial for your landing page to name your tiers according to their intended audience (i.e. Hobbyist, Developer, Pro instead of Standard, Premium, Deluxe).

No matter how your landing page is structured, you should feel free to modify, tweak, and improve your landing page as time goes on. As you learn new tricks and as you get feedback from users, go back and modify your landing page to make it better, more clear, and more understandable. Your landing page is the first chance you have to convince a potential user to sign up for your service or purchase your product. They say you never get a second chance at a first impression, and while that's technically true, every day on the Web you'll have the opportunity to give people a better first impression than you did the day before.

ADDING A KNOWLEDGE BASE

A knowledge base or wiki is an oft-overlooked but valuable part of any software service, and it serves a variety of uses. A knowledge base provides users with a centralized place containing answers to common questions, how-to guides, feature explanations, and legal and community standards documentation. A knowledge base also provides an opportunity for Content Marketing, which we'll cover later in this chapter. Suffice to say, providing a knowledge base for your users has a lot of important benefits. A knowledge base is a great way to explain your product or service to your users. Users often want to find out more about a service before signing up and handing over their personal information. Getting Started guides, Feature Spotlights and Testimonial pages can really help your users feel confident that they understand what your service does and encourages them to trust that you're not trying to scam them (which you shouldn't be). Additionally, your knowledge base can become a place where you explain or dive into detail about features or functionality that may not be intuitive for your users. If you find yourself constantly answering the same questions repeatedly in support emails, it might be time to publish an explainer article about that topic. These kinds of articles not only give you something to link to in your support emails, but they also provide users a way to answer some questions themselves.

PROMOTING YOUR WORK

Simply building a good, stable, useful product unfortunately just isn't enough to ensure your success. You need users. To get users you need to let people know about your product or service and convince them to click a link, sign up, and maybe even spend money. Convincing people en masse is challenging and time consuming, and it involves a certain amount of self-confidence to do well.

How you promote your work is up to you, and there are a vast array of options you can choose from. Each of these options requires you to be confident (or at least appear confident) in your work and in the value your product or service provides. Becoming comfortable with blatant self-confidence and self-promotion is a skill many people need to work hard to develop. I consider myself to be a confident person, but it still took a while before I was willing to publicly assert that my software was worth using at least without massive qualifications. Even though I believed my software was good and useful, I built it, so I saw the flaws, the imperfections, and the gaps left to fill. Marketing practices and social media platforms aren't conducive to nuanced conversations about niche markets and tradeoffs. You need to be confident (yet truthful) about the value your product or service provides, because that confidence directly transfers to the users you're trying to attract. After all, why should they have confidence in your product or service if you don't?

That said, confidence is only one part of being a successful promoter. The most confident tweet in the world won't necessarily reach a large enough audience to matter much. Volume and variety are at least as important.

You'll want to promote your work in a variety of different ways. The exact recipe is up to you, but you'll want to consider as many potential sources as possible to get the word out. These days it's incredibly common for products to have their own Facebook Pages, Twitter Accounts, Subreddits, Pinterest Boards, Blogs, Newsletters, and more. Your success with each of these will depend on your own dedication and knowledge of each source, and how each community using that source reacts to your product. Personally, I've had minimal success with Twitter; although, it's real-time nature makes it great for outage alerts or other immediate announcements. I've had essentially no success on Facebook. Reddit, on the other hand, has been incredibly useful, especially for Adventurer's Codex. The product's subreddit has remained fairly small, but Reddit also hosts a vibrant set of D&D communities that have been incredibly receptive to our work. Through it all though, the tools that have been most successful for me have been the least glamorous and the most old-school: blogs and email newsletters.

Blogs and newsletters can be incredibly important to your business because they're both methods of distribution that aren't controlled by another party. When someone signs up for your newsletter, they give you their email address and you send them alerts and announcements directly. Services like TinyLetter (which I've used many times and recommend highly) handle all of this for you. At their core, newsletters are the most direct method you have to tell your fans about new features or announcements. There's no algorithm deciding what your fans see, no company that decides what announcements are most engaging, and no middlemen between you and your fans.

Blogs fill a similar role. Like newsletters, they are public and give you a direct connection with your users. Additionally, they're easily searchable, posts can be easily cross-posted to services like Twitter and Facebook automatically, and Blogs act as a sort of record of past achievements. Newsletter fans will be ardent to point out that email newsletters can fill the same role (TinyLetter actually supports all of these features already), but blogs and landing pages are more Web-friendly and are often easier to discover and use by people browsing the Web. Blogs also cover a number of other responsibilities as well. In contrast with posting all of your announcements on social media platforms directly, hosting your releases and announcements on your own site gives you far more control over the format, content, and presentation. If you have a blog, you can write your releases and announcements there, and then have those announcements cross-posted to Twitter, Facebook, etc. These posts then usually link back to the original post on your business' blog. In this paradigm, social media platforms play more of a dissemination role. They distribute your release to users, but ultimately link back to your own site. This is really valuable for a number of reasons. Chief among them is that the traffic that comes from social media to your blog, will then help drive traffic to your product or service. Blogs also act as a record, a history of your product or service over time. This record is picked up by search engines and can increase traffic to your site over time.

Blogs and newsletters have a number of benefits. They provide you with a direct link to your customers and fans. They both improve your ranking with search engines. They can easily be configured to cross-post to social media platforms, saving you time and effort. And they are incredibly flexible and can be configured to fit your needs. The flexibility and power of blogs and newsletters has gone unappreciated for years as social media has become more and more prevalent and all encompassing, but that is slowly changing. As social media companies like Twitter and Facebook (and content distribution companies like YouTube) have gained power, many makers, developers, creators, and entrepreneurs are falling back to blogs and newsletters exactly because they offer that one main benefit: a direct connection with consumers. Some of the biggest channels on YouTube now rely on email newsletters and blogs to get the word out about new videos and projects precisely because YouTube's recommendation algorithm refuses to distribute their videos, even to those viewers who have subscribed to their channel or signed up for their notifications. In this increasingly algorithmic world, direct access to your user base is becoming ever more relevant to those who make things on the Web.[32] While you shouldn't ignore the giant social platforms, you shouldn't make them your only option either.

Overcoming the Fear of Blogging

Starting a blog can be intimidating, especially if you've never written a blog post before. The beauty of blogging is that it's informal. Blog posts aren't essays; they're casual and free-form. Release posts and announcements can be formal or informal, long or short, technical or targeted to a general audience. The details are up to you.

Blog posts for your product or service can be about anything you want. Use your blog to announce new features and releases, dive into a particular feature and explore how to use it and why, or explain to potential customers how your software solves a particular problem they might have. For example, if your service provides video hosting, explain why a YouTuber might find your service useful. If you provide uptime monitoring, like Nine9s, then explore why a developer would choose your service over a competitor. In some cases, the reader doesn't even know what your service is. You can use your blog, in conjunction with your knowledge base, to explain what your service is and why someone would use it. If you're feeling brave and committal, then talk about the features you're working on now that haven't launched yet. Not only does this build hype and excitement, it lets users know what's coming and humanizes your business.

Like I said, these posts don't need to be long or extensive. As developer and business owner Gina Trapani wrote on her blog in 2014, "If it's a paragraph, it's a post. Medium-sized content gets short shrift these days. Don't go long. One or two paragraphs count. Then press publish."[33] Once you have a blog post published, let your subscribers know. Send out an email to your newsletter subscribers, include a brief snippet from the blog post, and then link back to the post directly. Make sure to cross-post what you just wrote to Social media, and include a link there as well. It may sound intimidating, but promoting yourself this way is incredibly powerful. It takes time to build an audience, and it takes patience and the willingness to fail in public. You may publish a post with glaring typos, or fail to meet a goal you publicly set in a previous post. That's ok. Be honest with your readers. Correct the mistakes and update your commitments. Learn from your mistakes and work towards getting better. Your audience will appreciate your honesty and sincerity.

Blogging and the Long Tail

Blog posts aren't like tweets or Facebook posts. They stick around and they're indexed by search engines. Just like the content on your homepage, your blog posts serve an ulterior motive: they drive traffic to your service. We often think that posts get most of their views in the first few days after they're released. That's when we're talking about them, promoting them, and that's when they're the freshest in our own mind. But in reality, this simply isn't true. Because they stick around forever (assuming you don't delete them), blog posts accumulate traffic over time. Blog posts usually attract traffic according to the power law distribution. If you'll excuse the statistics lesson for a minute, the power law (sometimes referred to as the scaling law) states that a relative change in one value (time), results in a proportional relative change in another (traffic). Think of it this way, once you release a blog post and share it with people, it will start to get noticed. The thing is, your blog post's relevance doesn't disappear the next day, it stays roughly the same. Each day that goes by, your post becomes a little less relevant (but not irrelevant), and a new post doesn't degrade the quality of older ones. Most blog post traffic follows a trend like this:

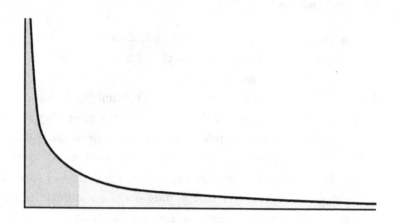

Power law - Wikipedia https://en.wikipedia.org/wiki/Power_law

In our blogging example, the horizontal axis represents time since publication and the vertical axis is traffic. As you can see, the more recent the post, the more traffic it gets. The relevance and traffic that a single page gets over time drops rapidly at the start, and most people intuitively believe that after a certain point, that specific post stops driving traffic. There is, however, a quirk of the power law distribution. Notice how the graph is shaded, one side dark and one light. Both of those shaded areas are of equal size. This means that a post that attracts 5000 pageviews in the first chunk of time will likely attract another 5000 more. Effectively, this means that your blog posts remain useful long after they're published, as long as they aren't deleted. Every blog post you write increases your exposure. To this day, the posts that are the most popular overall on my personal blog are posts I wrote years ago. More recent posts are usually more popular in the current moment, but older posts are still consistently driving traffic to my site years after they were published.

This is the hidden power of blogging in marketing. Posts that were initially popular tend to remain fairly popular over time.

People are looking for answers and services all the time, not just on the day you publish a post. In this way, blog posts are a tacit advertising campaign. As people search for relevant answers to their questions, your blog posts drive them to your site without you having done anything at all.

CONTENT MARKETING

Your blog and knowledge base are two important opportunities for your business. Both tend to drive traffic to your site, and both aim to get users interested in your product or service. On the surface, release blog posts are useful because they are where your existing users can access the details of the new release, and your knowledge base is useful because it can help users get answers to questions. Both also serve as vectors for Content Marketing.

Content Marketing is a marketing technique that takes into account the fact that people are constantly asking questions on the Web and using search engines to answer them. Traditional marketing techniques are aimed at users looking to purchase a product and try to convince the potential user that the product is superior to the competition. Content Marketing is a little different. Say you're looking for a recipe for vegetarian tikka masala and you find a helpful recipe with great tips and easy to follow instructions. That recipe might be hosted on a site that sells cookware. By helping you find information that is genuinely useful, the seller has also convinced you to visit their site, where they can provide links to sell cookware used in the dish they're describing. Content Marketing can also take the form of documentation. Linode is a great example of this. The company puts out lots of technical documentation. That documentation is well written and serves as a resource to everyone on the internet, not just its own customers. This means that after reading their excellent documentation, readers may decide to trust Linode and sign up for hosting. Your blog and knowledge base fill the same role. By posting about new features on your blog, or writing explainer articles using your knowledge base, you are partly educating existing users, and also casting a wider net to catch some new users as well. The goal of Content Marketing isn't to be deceitful (though some companies are). Try to be helpful and insightful. If you have ideas or thoughts about topics related to your company's product or service, then write about them. Adventurer's Codex, for example, is a web app that's designed to help players keep track of their D&D characters and campaigns. Each of us are enthusiastic D&D players and we'd noticed that the community was conflicted over whether to allow phones and tablets during games because they can be distracting. We all believed it was possible that those devices can improve, rather than detract from, playing D&D. So, we wrote a blog post about how we play using Adventurer's Codex on laptops and tablets during our games, and we explored rules that others could implement if they wanted to add electronic devices to their games, in a non-distracting way.[34] Over the years we explored a number of other topics ranging from new kinds of house-rules to crafting and role-playing characters. Pine.blog has done similar things. Like I've said before, Pine.blog is a feed reader and blogging platform. A lot of people don't even know what a feed reader is or what they can do. To address this, the Pine.blog knowledge base has a number of articles targeted at anyone looking to learn more about feed readers and blogging, not just targeted at Pine.blog users. Content Marketing is incredibly beneficial when used properly. It's both a marketing technique that attracts users and improves the community by providing guidance and helpful explanations to users all across the Web.

MANAGING YOUR IMAGE

How you write on your site is (of course) up to you. That said, there are two general forms that your writing can take, and each one has its own benefits and drawbacks. For example, you may be tempted to write your announcement posts, knowledge base articles, and support pages in an impersonal corporate tone. This style is common among big businesses. The tone combines enthusiasm with professionalism, and can be utilized to create the impression that your business is bigger and more important than it actually is, which can be advantageous. Apple uses this kind of tone a lot. Consider this quote, taken from one of Apple's latest press releases.

> Apple today announced that Phil Schiller will become an Apple Fellow, continuing a storied career that began at Apple in 1987. In this role, which reports to Apple CEO Tim Cook, Schiller will continue to lead the App Store and Apple Events. Greg (Joz) Joswiak, a longtime leader within the Product Marketing organization, will join the executive team as senior vice president of Worldwide Marketing.

The release is written in the third person, they never refer to themselves as "we" or "us", instead saying "Apple". This makes the press release sound impartial or objective. The release also conveys confidence, and phrases like, "continuing a storied career", and "longtime leader" impart a sense of momentum to the occasion.

Often, when using this technique, updates are written in passive voice. In these cases, the writer is merely describing events like a journalist, not actively participating in them. Articles that do this read more like a newspaper column than a blog post. This style may allow you to portray your business and products as professional and enterprise-level. You may successfully convince people that your company is actually bigger and more important than it is, but you also convey the impression that your software is stable and powerful, developed by competent professionals, not whimsical amateurs. Portraying yourself as a big, important, professional company might be the best bet for your goals, niche, or customers; however, the approach does have its downsides. First off, it can be surprisingly difficult to write in this style if you're not accustomed to it. The language feels rigid, academic, and unemotional, which can make building enthusiasm difficult. Second, and what I've found most relevant, is that customers act surprisingly different when contacting or reaching out to large companies versus small ones. In my experience, if customers expect that your company has a fully staffed, byzantine customer support department, they tend to expect responses sooner and will be more hostile in the conversation. They're on guard; expecting the company to try to punt responsibility or waste their time. Despite the cons, for some this style will be necessary. If your business sells services to other large companies or manages expensive contracts, then those clients will expect a measure of professionalism from you, your documentation and your public notices. On the other hand, if you're targeting a more consumer-friendly market or the general public, you may consider ditching the professional airs entirely.

Instead of pursuing a formal enterprise image, a lot of independent developers choose to conduct themselves in a much more casual, informal, and personal way. A lot of time this will mean including casual language and your own name. Marco

Arment, maker of the popular podcast app Overcast, has discussed this approach multiple times on his podcast and blog. Arment tends to favor casual language in his app and on his site. Consider this example, taken from Overcast's contact page, and contrast it with the earlier statement from Apple.

> Hi, I'm Marco Arment. I run Overcast with no other employees, no VC funding, and a sustainable work-life balance (hopefully) so I can spend enough time with my family. Nice to meet you.
>
> I'm a software developer, writer, podcaster, and huge podcast fan. I talked about why I love podcasts and why I made Overcast during this XOXO 2013 presentation.

This language, casual and straightforward, sets the stage for users who might be seeking help or looking for a place to request features or report bugs. Arment has said on his podcast, the Accidental Tech Podcast (ATP), that this blurb (situated directly above the instructions for contacting him) helps diffuse tensions and has resulted in less combative and more compassionate support emails. Arment also claims that providing customers insights into the workings of his business (i.e. having one employee, working to support his family, working to sustain a healthy work-life balance, etc) has helped manage expectations resulting in a better experience for both parties. I've found this to be true as well in my own work. Adventurer's Codex originally tried to convey the impression that it was a bigger business than the reality, while Pine.blog never attempted such a thing. To this day, Adventurer's Codex receives (on average) more confrontational support emails than Pine.blog. This casual approach can help you as a business owner feel more comfortable too. You may find it difficult or feel pretentious writing in such a formal or enterprise-y way, and a more casual format may encourage you to write more and write more often. Authenticity is not the same thing as unprofessionalism, which can cause users to consider you dismissive or unreliable. The main downside to authenticity is that users will expect you to be authentic, even when things go wrong. They'll expect insights, explanations, and reasons when you mess up. If your company gives off formal airs, you can probably get away with more vague, less committal language. When you mess up, users will expect an apology. They'll expect you to be transparent and forthcoming. Learning to apologize in public is hard and it can be incredibly stressful, but that sincerity can also reward you. There are few things less trustworthy than a business trying to appear transparent and authentic, while hiding behind a veil of formality when they make mistakes or are challenged on their decisions. If you choose the casual, honest route, your users will trust you because they know that you'll tell them when you mess up. Though, if you decide to be truly authentic, you need to own it 100% of the time.

Whether you choose to come off as a formal big business, or strive to be more personal with your users, is up to you. The important thing is that you consider what image you would like your company to portray, and then be consistent. Once you've decided to go down a certain path, stick to it. Customers and potential users will notice the inconsistencies and they could mistakenly interpret those changes in tone as a lack of commitment or quality. You can obviously change course if the path you've chosen is uncomfortable or no longer makes sense, but under normal circumstances it's best to pick one voice and develop it. Writing in a given style or voice is hard, and it takes time to develop your own skills in a medium. Don't fault yourself when you fail to stick to your voice. Analyze your writing style, figure out your mistakes, and try to do better next time.

Writing is a process, not a destination. Your goal in writing is to communicate with your users, and hopefully convince some of those who stumble upon your posts to join up. No blog post will ever be perfect, but they don't need to be. They need to be informative and clear.

GETTING NOTICED

Before anyone can discover your product, or stumble across your blog and knowledge base, your site needs to be discovered by search engines and added to their indexes. Given enough time, search engines like Google and Bing will eventually discover your site on their own, but it's faster and easier if you let them know about it directly. Both Google and Bing provide webmaster portals which allow site owners to add their site to their search indexes. Whats more, when you add your site directly, both services provide you with a dashboard that shows how many searches have resulted in your site appearing in the results and how many times someone then clicked on your site from those results.

We'll be focusing exclusively on Google and Bing for the remainder of this section because, in 2020, they are the only two U.S. search engines that still actively crawl the Web and build their own search indexes. All other search engines purchase data and results from these two providers and combine them with data purchased from other providers.

You can find the Google and Bing Webmaster tools here:

- www.google.com/webmasters/
- www.bing.com/toolbox/webmaster/

For each service, you'll need to create and verify an account before you can add your site. You'll also need to configure some DNS TXT records to prove to both Google and Bing that you do in fact own the domain or website that you're trying to claim. Once you do all of that you'll be able to browse graphs and data that detail how each search engine is displaying your site in their results, and how many people are clicking on those results.

The Google Webmaster Performance Dashboard

Both the Google and Bing dashboards update very slowly. Results may take up to three days before appearing in the dashboard. That said, the dashboards aren't the thing we're after. They're just a nice side-effect. Most importantly, by registering with both Google and Bing, your site will now appear in their search results (after a few days, of course).

Now that your site is included in Google and Bing's index, you can further help their algorithms understand the structure of your site. You can do this with two key tools: a robots.txt file and a sitemap. Robots.txt files are simple text files served at a standard path that let Web crawlers know what content they should ignore and what content you would like crawled. Robots.txt directives are enforced entirely through the honor-system, but both Google and Bing, as well as a host of other well-behaved crawlers, obey the rules you specify. Sitemaps on the other hand are XML files that list popular or common pages. Sitemaps help search engines discover as many pages on your site as possible and allow them to forgo crawling your entire site to discover random pages. Sitemaps are incredibly easy to implement, and most Web frameworks have plug-ins that can generate them for you. Once you've generated a sitemap, add it to your site's profile in the Google and Bing Webmaster dashboards and their crawlers will start to leverage it.

If you're using the Django Web framework, you can easily add one or multiple sitemaps to your site automatically using the built-in sitemap generation tools. As with so much in the Django world, what's necessary for a good site comes included in the framework.

IMPROVING YOUR CHANCES

Just because your site appears in search results on Google and Bing doesn't mean that it appears near the top. Like most things on the Web, search traffic decays exponentially. Exponential decay looks pretty similar to the curve we saw in our discussion of blogging's long tail. The first result gets a large number of clicks, the second gets significantly less, and traffic goes to near zero for sites listed after the first page. Search results are ordered by a hidden ranking, and while the criteria and ranking system is different for different search engines, the basics are shared between them. In abstract, sites are included in search results if they're deemed relevant to the user's query. Those relevant sites are then ranked according to a number of criteria that are used to judge how trustworthy, reliable, and popular a given site is. The more relevant, the more popular, or the more trustworthy a site is, the higher its ranking and thus the closer to the top it appears. Your job is to optimize the content on your public pages to ensure that you're following the best practices from each of the search providers, and to convince other popular or prominent sites to link to your site in order to boost your ranking and drive more traffic to your site.

Typically speaking, a well optimized site can get more, and more consistent, traffic from search results than from almost any other audience acquisition method. Advertising, marketing, and word of mouth are all incredibly useful tools and they can help encourage people to check out your site, but they can be difficult to obtain. Word-of-mouth promotion takes a long time to develop and a passionate user-base willing to spread the word. Advertising is expensive, and marketing takes a lot of time and effort. Traffic from search results, on the other hand, is directly driven by users searching for exactly the thing you're selling. By definition, if a person is searching for your product or service, they're more likely to spend money or sign up when compared to a person who had no prior interest in your product or service until they saw an ad, and therefore your search ranking is arguably more important than any advertising you could ever do. Luckily there are ways to improve your search ranking, and they're pretty straightforward to implement.

Search Engine Optimization or SEO is a practice that uses a number of guidelines put out by search providers combined with a variety of heuristics and assumptions about the inner workings of search ranking systems to improve the ranking of a given site. SEO is sometimes dismissed as cheating since the site owner is deliberately altering their site to get more traffic, and while some sites do try to scam or trick the search ranking algorithms into promoting their site for almost any query, most SEO tips and tricks are actually just good Web design practices. Search providers build their algorithms to recommend things users actually want to see. If a search engine was easily scammed or served results that didn't match the user's question then people would stop using it. At their most simple and virtuous, search providers want to accurately answer a user's question. If you believe you have a good answer or solution for a wide swath of users, then it's useful to let the search provider know that so they can recommend your site to their users. There are a lot of great SEO tools out there these days that can help you improve your site's SEO score. Keep in mind though, these scores are all hypothetical. Google and Bing won't tell you your actual score. They keep most of their ranking systems close to the chest. The SEO industry is taking the little information they do release and reading the tea leaves to figure out the rest.

In general, SEO best practices are pretty simple: pages should be relatively small, they should load quickly, your web server should return useful cache directives, any images should be compressed and scaled to the proper size, CSS and Javascript files should be minified, HTML title and description tags should contain useful information, your site should use standard markup like h1 and h2 tags for titles and subtitles, your pages should reuse and promote common phrases or terms, your site should include titles for links and alt text for images, and if your site contains Javascript, that code shouldn't throw exceptions. All of these things are just plain good practice. That said, it's common, especially in development, to forget to do many of these things. You may have a very fast home internet connection or you're serving assets locally, and therefore you may not notice that one of your icons is actually a 12MB image that you forgot to resize and compress. Link titles and image alt-texts are invisible on the rendered page and easy to overlook, but forgetting to add them can make your site less SEO friendly and hinder your site's usability for people with slow connections or those who need screen readers or other accessibility tools.

While most SEO guidelines are pretty simple, straightforward, and obviously beneficial, some SEO tools will recommend practices that, in my view, are antithetical to the goals I have. You shouldn't just blindly adopt the recommendations and practices listed on any given SEO website. Before you make any changes that are either significant in scope or that don't have an obvious practical benefit, consider whether the recommendation is valuable or not. Most SEO scoring tools are free, but they're made by companies wanting you to sign up for more SEO insights or tools. These companies may not share your values and therefore might recommend things that go against your principles. As an example: Most SEO scoring tools will recommend that you include social media share buttons or other social integrations on your site, and we know from disclosures, that those buttons and integrations track visitor behavior even when they aren't clicked. This enables companies like Google, Facebook, and Twitter to track your users while they use your site. Personally, I find ad-tracking and other similar practices like this to be incredibly distasteful, so I don't include those buttons on any of my sites. This affects my SEO score, but it does so in a way I'm comfortable with.

Good SEO combined with a good content marketing strategy and a regularly updated blog can drastically improve your search ranking and lead to large amounts of daily traffic. Lots of traffic then helps people discover your site and your software which makes it easier for word-of-mouth to spread. This virtuous cycle builds on itself to your benefit. Adventurer's Codex was able to cultivate this virtuous cycle and the results boosted the site's popularity more than any other technique we tried. After we built out the initial app and landing page, we delved into making a blog and writing explainer pages that provided details about the software, how it worked, and how it could improve the experience of playing D&D. These pages explained the app's features from the perspective of players, DMs, and entire parties (i.e. everyone playing at the session). After a few months of moderate growth, we noticed that traffic had begun to spike and our analytics and surveys showed that a disproportionate number of our users were DMs. We knew that there were far fewer options for DM tools in the community, but since there are, on average, three to four players per DM in a game of D&D, this was pretty unexpected. We soon discovered that while a Google search for "D&D player tools" ranked us in the top 25 results, a search for "D&D DM tools" returned our site in the number one or number two spot consistently. Our SEO and content marketing strategy worked. For over two years, searches for "D&D DM tools" on Google would return our site in the top five. This resulted in thousands of clicks and page-views each month. To this day, that listing did more for us than any other promotional tactic, and it can do the same for you.

A THORNY TOPIC: ADS

Let's talk about ads. There are multiple kinds of ads on the Web: display, search, podcast, pre-roll video, and more. Each of these ads have different benefits and drawbacks, but for the purposes of this discussion, we're going to focus on the kinds of ads that are the most prevalent and the most inexpensive: display and search ads. Over the years I've purchased a fair number of ads, both for Adventurer's Codex and for SkyRocket Software. I've tweaked each platform differently, tried multiple strategies, and attempted to leverage the power of each ad platform to their fullest. So in this section, we're going to dive into what I've learned, what strategies worked (and what didn't), and then discuss some criteria you can use to judge whether purchasing ads is a good idea for your business. But before we can dive too deep, let's quickly go over how these ads work and what benefits they claim to have.

Ad networks, like Google, Facebook, Reddit, Twitter, Yahoo, and others, allow businesses to buy advertising space on their platforms, or on their partner's platforms, and they either show those ads on their platform or they provide website owners with simple integrations to present their ads for a share in the revenue. For example, if I'm a popular blogger and I'd like to earn some income from my writing, I can choose to include ads from Google on my site. These display ads, are served by Google and include content from the business that purchased the ad. Display ads are mostly targeted at users who are visiting an unrelated site. Technically speaking, companies like Google use their user data (search history, interests, demographic information, and more) to target their display ads to the specific users they believe are most likely to click on them. Display ads are typically inexpensive, but this is largely because they are also notoriously ineffective They have a very low click-though rate (i.e. the number of times someone clicks the ad and visits the page), which is partly due to the fact that most ad-blockers simply remove them from the page entirely, but also because they are just plain annoying.

Display Ads vs. Search Ads

Search ads, on the other hand, appear at the top of Google search results. These ads can be customized to appear based on any number of keywords or phrases, and they show up only for users that are already explicitly searching for the thing being advertised. Search ads can be significantly more effective than display ads because, when done well, a user is hopefully already looking for a service or software like yours, and all the search ads do is move your product to the top of the list of results. Search ads are not typically removed by ad-blockers and are not obnoxious in terms of placement or design. That said, most people have "ad-blindness", meaning that even though they see the ads, most users don't register their contents or read them at all; instead they scan the page for the first "real" search result and start their browsing there. This is yet another reason why good SEO is far more important than a good ad campaign.

There are many problems with Web ads, and I won't go into them here. Suffice to say that, as I mentioned above, ads are a tool that allow companies to track user behavior across the Web. Adding display ads to your site, advertising with the big ad networks, or even just adding social media share buttons to your site forces you to confront this behavior.

Search ads can be optimized and targeted at users looking for a specific product or service. This is useful because it allows your ads to appear in front of users looking to purchase the exact thing you're selling. You can also target searches related to your software or your knowledge base. You may find, for example that users don't usually search for your software by name or they might not know how to describe the kind of software you're offering. Nine9s has this issue. Technically Nine9s is an uptime-monitoring service, but even knowledgeable developers don't search for services using those terms. In this case, you may want to target keywords like "outage" or "downtime" which are more common descriptors. In other cases you may want to advertise the content of your knowledge base. You may discover that visitors find one of your articles incredibly valuable, perhaps an explainer page or a how-to page. In those cases you can advertise and promote that page directly and use that opportunity to direct users to try out your service once they're done reading the article.

Often times companies will target search ads using keywords that describe their competitors. For example, Nine9s may want to target users searching for Pingdom, a popular uptime-monitoring service. This practice is incredibly common and it's the reason why you may search for a popular product by name and get results for a different, but similar, product first.

Personally, while this tactic might be incredibly common, it still feels gross to me. You're effectively trying to siphon traffic from competitors directly. I have targeted ads using the names of competitors in the past and felt bad doing so, but since I don't use search ads anymore, my aversion to this problem has mostly solved itself.

In my experience, display ads have proven to be entirely a waste of money, and search ads yield mixed results. On a few occasions, they've resulted in significant traffic, while most times they have been entirely useless. None of my search ad campaigns have been profitable; they've always resulted in a net-loss. I can't say your products will have the same result, but it does seem that search ads may only be useful with enough volume over time, and that drastically increases the cost of the ad campaign beyond what a small business can typically afford. Because of this, I can't recommend either display or search ads as cost effective ways to promote your software. The benefits of good SEO and organic promotion can't be replicated by typical Web advertising methods. If you are tempted to try anyways, you could potentially experiment with search ads, but only if you have the money to burn. Like gambling, when you pay for advertising, you shouldn't spend any money you aren't willing to lose with no return. If you have that extra money in your budget, before experimenting with search ads I would actually recommend considering a higher quality format like podcast ads. These are significantly more expensive than Web ads, but appear to have a much higher rate of return and, when done well, come with none of the drawbacks for either you or the listeners.

Preparing for Launch

There are a lot of ways to launch software. Of course, you can just wake up, kick on the server, send out a tweet, and be done with it, but a successful launch usually involves significantly more work. You can't launch your software twice, so you need to plan ahead and try to ensure your one shot goes as well as possible. Before you launch, you'll need to verify that your software works well and isn't filled with nasty bugs, you'll need to shore up any legal documents and ensure your software complies with relevant laws and regulations, you'll need to get people interested and convince them to follow your blog or sign up for your newsletter, and you may want to see if you can garner some press coverage. A lot of this work is time consuming and your results will vary drastically depending on your approach, so it's equally important to set your own expectations to match the situation. A lot of the work you do before you launch will build up the event in your own mind. This internal hype is important because it can be a powerful motivator, driving you to contact more people and garner more interest, but that hype can also be your biggest downfall. If you build up your launch day too much, even the best launches can feel incredibly disappointing.

In this section, we'll look at a few things you should consider when preparing to launch your software, what things you'll need to finalize beforehand, and how to get people paying attention when you do finally launch. Like marketing, a good launch will require you to be creative, and to think about promoting yourself and your software in clever ways. As developers on the Web, we are often blinded by our own industry practices. Sometimes we start believing that the only way to get something done is on the Web itself, but as we'll see in this section, a successful launch may involve reaching far beyond the comforts of the Web and into the real world. You may find that a Web-only promotional strategy works for you, but you may also find that an offline promotion works just as well if not better.

That said, lot's of books and blog posts talk about how to promote your software, and how to launch. They work to convince you that if you do what they say, everything will be great and your launch will be a magnificent success, but those same books, posts, and podcasts conveniently gloss over the ever-real possibility that your launch fails to attract significant attention. Importantly though, a launch's success is entirely determined by your own expectations. If you expect it to attract 50 people and it attracts 500, then that's a success, but if you expect 50,000 and only see 10,000 on launch day, then you may consider that a failure even if (by most measures) you did very well. With that in mind, we'll also look at some real data from my own attempts to launch software. Hopefully this should provide some context to help define a "successful" launch.

Always remember that launching software isn't a science. It's not a reproducible experiment; there are no do-overs and so much of the success of your launch is dependent on factors outside of your control. But there are a few things you can do to better your chances, and help ensure your launch goes well. With effort (and some luck) your launch can be the kickstart your business needs.

BETA TESTING AND SOFT LAUNCH

The goal of both a beta testing phase and a soft launch are pretty similar. Both periods allow users to use your service and provide feedback before you announce your software to the world and the general public. Both techniques are valuable, and while you may find that you don't need one phase or the other, having both a beta testing phase and a soft launch period allow you to better ensure the quality of your software at launch-time and help you build hype for your software's eventual release.

Beta testing is a pretty common phase of the software development process. Typically, software in beta isn't yet ready for a wide audience, but the core of the software exists and can be tested, critiqued, and improved. The software at this stage may still contain significant bugs or lack critical features. If you decide to do a beta testing phase, you'll first want to decide what kind of beta testing you want to do. Open betas are available to the public or some specific sector, while closed betas are limited to specific people or involve an invite process. Open beta participation might be limited to a certain finite number of users, but generally speaking those users can come from anywhere and there's little if any vetting or approval needed to join an open beta program. Generally, closed betas are less effective than open betas because of the sheer numbers involved. Since closed betas are usually pretty small, the amount of traffic or testing your software will get is minimal, but the quality of feedback is usually higher. Asking your friends and family to review and try your software is a simple example of a closed beta. Open betas will test more of your software, but you'll need testing and reporting systems in place to catch and track most bugs since open beta users are far less likely to actually report issues. Either type of beta phase can be incredibly useful, as testers tend to try execution paths you wouldn't often consider or don't regularly test. This does mean that you need good people testing your software; and, for a good beta testing phase, those good people actually need to report their issues to you. Finding these people is perhaps the most significant challenge with beta testing, regardless of the style.

Soft launches, which are common practice in other industries, are an often under-appreciated technique in the software industry. A soft launch is essentially just a regular launch but without the promotion. Restaurants do this all the time. The restaurant will open its doors to passing customers, affording them the opportunity to test their processes, try menu items, and get feedback on the decor before opening the restaurant officially. While an official launch may garner press and be accompanied by massive social media blitzes or even a sizable ad campaign, a soft launch just happens, silently or with very little promotion. By entering a soft launch period, you allow users to sign up for your service and you give yourself breathing room to test out features and ideas with a small testing cohort, while also minimizing the damage if something goes wrong. Importantly, soft launches reduce the stress of your actual promoted launch significantly, since you already know that the software that you're launching works and works well. You don't need to worry about outages, downtime, or massive day-one bugs and you can instead focus on promotion efforts.

Whether you decide to do either a soft launch or a limited beta testing phase (or both) these techniques are aimed at ensuring a successful launch and minimizing the accompanying stress of launch day. No matter which method you choose, set up some way for users to get in contact with you to report issues. These methods should be as non-technical and approachable as possible. In the past, I've used both Slack and Discord to allow for launch day or release day feedback. Slack in particular is incredibly helpful for this because it's already adopted by a large number of companies for their internal use. Many people will already have accounts on Slack which makes the onboarding process for your beta testers or soft launch users much easier.

IMPROVING THROUGH USER FEEDBACK

Your ability to gain feedback from your users doesn't stop when you launch. Just because you're not in a beta testing phase or soft launch doesn't mean you can't gather user feedback, but it does affect the methods by which you ask for that feedback and what kinds of questions you should consider asking. Since launch, Adventurer's Codex has included two short, optional surveys. After a user creates their account, an email is sent with an account activation link, as standard practice would dictate. Immediately after sending (but before informing them of the email), we ask the user two simple questions: "How did you hear about Adventurer's Codex", and "What kind of player are you?" with the answers of either Player, Dungeon Master (i.e. the person running the game), or Both. On the second survey, which a user can opt to take at any time from their account profile page, we ask the user about the device they prefer to use with the software, what they enjoy most about the product, how they use it, and what improvements they'd like to see. These two surveys have gotten thousands of responses over the years and the answers in them have guided product decisions and helped us better understand how people use the software day-to-day. Interestingly, leaving aside people who discover the service through Google search queries, our users report that their friends and family are the most common source of referrals. This captures a metric that traffic monitoring services just can't hope to extract.

Social media, chat rooms, and community forums are another way you can solicit feedback from your users. The Adventurer's Codex subreddit and Discord have both been useful for this, as has the private Pine.blog beta tester Slack group. Each of these tools allow your users to get in contact with you. Personally, I tend to prefer older, less platform-specific methods like email, but such things aren't really searchable or public, like subreddits. These channels also allow your users to communicate with each other and share tips, information, or confirm issues. In the olden days, software services might have an accompanying forum site or IRC channel for exactly this purpose, and subreddits fulfill a similar role today.

When collecting user feedback from surveys, emails, and social media it's important to remember that you should take these suggestions with a grain of salt. By definition, the users that are the most passionate, the most invested, the most happy (or the most angry) about your software are the people writing these comments. Their wants and needs may not reflect the feelings of your user base at large. Over time, as you collect more and more feedback, you may notice that some enormous percentage of that feedback is asking for essentially the same feature, and you may be tempted to build that feature. Of course, it might be true that said feature would significantly enhance your product, but before you let your users make such a decision, consult the other aspects of your business. Does this feature make strategic sense? Does it further your other goals? How much time would it take to build? All of these and more are important considerations. User feedback is a valuable tool to aid your decision-making process, but it's not the only one.

Let's look at an example of how you can leverage user feedback. Let's say you've narrowed down a list of features and you're looking to prioritize them. In this case, user feedback can be helpful. If your users want one of those features more than another, then you can use that information to rank the features on your priority list. That said, you shouldn't outsource your product decisions to your users in any significant way. As we covered in our discussion of the different hats you wear as a business owner, users don't tend to think of the business aspects of a decision or the ways certain features would fit into the business' strategic vision of the product. If you can, collect user feedback, but don't let it overpower your decisions.

HANDLING LEGALITIES

While small internet companies with under 10,000 users and little revenue are rarely the subject of direct legal requirements, there are still a few important things you need to do before your software can be released to the world. A lot of these requirements are technically optional, but you'll want to put yourself and your business on the best possible legal and ethical footing going into your launch. Many developers find these legal or business items to be confusing or intimidating, but like with many things they get easier once you understand the requirements and the terminology.

The two most common and important documents you'll need to craft are your Terms of Service and Privacy Policy. Templates for both of these documents can be found online and can be easily tweaked to suit your needs. A Terms of Service document is an agreement that the users must agree to abide by in order to use your software. A ToS document often describes how a service can or can't be used and includes language allowing your business to administer and moderate your service. For example, you may reserve the right to close any account at any time, or you may choose to enforce a code of conduct that users must obey. Crucially, your ToS should explain your policies and allow users to contact you for clarification and complaints regarding the terms. Similarly, a Privacy Policy simply explains to your users what kinds of data you collect and how you plan to use that data. If your service collects behavioral data, then you'll need to disclose that. In most cases you don't need to be too specific and you can give yourself flexibility to change your process without updating the Privacy Policy, but you should make the policy specific enough to give users some insights into what you're doing with their data. Nine9s and Pine.blog collect no behavioral data and only leverage the data directly entered by users or supplied by the HTTP specification that's needed for service administration (i.e. IP address, etc). Your Privacy Policy should also explain how long you keep the data you collect, and how users can request the removal or deletion of that data. If your software is subject to GDPR and CCPA provisions, then you'll need to obtain consent from your users before you can collect their data and expressly commit to purging data once a user has requested it. These processes can be manual, there's no requirement that a user be able to simply click a button to have their data deleted, though that is obviously preferred. You can simply ask users to email you and request their data be deleted. If your process is automatic, you'll want to ensure your users that their data is removed in a timely manner. Data stored in system backups may not be removed immediately and may take time to rotate through the system. Give your users insight into when their data will be fully removed.

Data Retention is an important aspect to consider when designing your systems, and an explicit data retention policy is often a requirement for larger companies, and one you should strive to imitate. Let's look at a simple example of a data retention policy and explore what it means and what business impact the policy might have. Let's say that your software tracks and logs the page-views for every logged in user in an effort to better understand how your users navigate your software. While I'd argue that most anonymous methods for doing so are good enough, let's say your service tracks this information and explicitly associates it with the user's account. Even the most extensive and effective optimization system won't require the page-view data for every user from every point in the past. The page-view data has a usable life after which the data is effectively useless or redundant. If your site hasn't changed in months, then user behavioral data from yesterday is likely just as useful as data from two months ago. Similarly, if your site went through a site-wide reorganization recently, the data from before the reorg is useless now because the pages and the content on each page is different, so the corresponding user behavior will also have changed. Either way, the usefulness of this behavioral data decays over time. A lot of companies will simply store and archive this data, which again has no practical use anymore. In this case, the proper thing to do is delete it. Not only will this reduce overall storage costs, but it allows you to promise your users that you're not keeping their data beyond the point when you need it. This same policy applies to all kinds of data your system collects. Pine.blog tracks the incidents of background-task failure at a fairly granular level to allow for debugging of complex and often invisible issues, but this data is deleted after 30 days. Most times, bugs are resolved within that period and after the bug is fixed, there's no need for the diagnostic data used to debug it. In other cases, the issue is the result of global networking issues or problems with an external origin site which resolve themselves over time. Either way, there's no need to store and hold this data beyond the 30 day retention period. Once you have a data retention policy in place, explain the policy to your users in your Privacy Policy.

This all may sound intimidating, but it doesn't have to be. These documents are often written in complex legalese, but that's not a requirement, especially when your company is small. Explain yourself, your policies, and your process simply and clearly. Provide disclaimers where you can and explain that your service complies with the laws as you understand them. The goal of these documents is to provide your users with knowledge to help them understand how their data is used, what your service provides, and what is expected of them in return. Small companies that use plain-language contracts are often held to a different standard than large companies with legal teams. Be honest, be transparent, and follow the examples of other companies in the same space.

Notes on Data Collection & Legal Requirements

The following section does not constitute legal advice. I am not a lawyer. Instead, the goal of this section is to provide you with a broad overview of the general legal requirements and industry-standard best practices as I understand them. Please do your own research and ensure your particular app or service complies with all relevant laws and regulations. When it comes to GDPR specifically, there are lots of great resources including blogs, podcasts, and more by knowledgeable people who can guide you through the process of ensuring that your app or service is compliant.

Most likely you will already have a data model by the time you construct your Privacy Policy and Terms of Service. When you're designing that model, consider what data you want to collect from your users and why you want that data. In general, your software should only collect information you absolutely need for your business, and you should always provide your users with some basic information about how the data you collect will be used. A lot of this is just good design, but some is also legally required. The General Data Protection Regulation (GDPR) is a European Union regulation that applies to all Internet services that serve European customers, regardless of the business' location. This means that all companies that serve European customers must comply, and since our service is on the Web and we don't block European IP addresses (which isn't sufficient anyway) we too, must comply. Essentially, the GDPR, and California's Consumer Privacy Act (CCPA) are designed to protect consumers from predatory actions by businesses that collect and sell their users' data. If you're not engaged in such activity, your service is largely exempt from these regulations.

That said, there are things that you are recommended or required to do to disclose what you do with user data.

While this may seem burdensome or complex, the GDPR and CCPA doesn't actually require most Internet services to do very much. Both are mostly concerned with Data Providers and Data Brokers, which are businesses that sell or provide access to user data, and those that buy, collect, or use that data in ways that don't directly serve the needs of users using the service. If you're not doing any of those things, and providing a service for a fee, there's not much you need to do. In these cases, to comply, you simply need to inform your users of how you use their data and have them agree that they understand and approve. Certain kinds of data, especially personal information like real names, addresses, and demographic information are considered protected personal information data and fall under different regulations. If your app collects any of this information you will want to investigate how these laws govern your use of that data. Nine9s collects an account email address and password as well as Alert Contact information including additional email addresses and phone numbers. Payment information is handled through an external provider, and no data is ever sold or transferred outside of the system. If your service collects different or more personal kinds of information, you may need to do more to comply with these laws and regulations.

GETTING PRESS

During the beta testing process, you should consider reaching out to prominent blogs and bloggers to see if they'd be interested in reviewing your product on release day. Sites like iMore, Android Central, TechCrunch, Engadget, MacStories, and others regularly review and promote new apps and services when they launch. Even a mention by such a prominent site can boost your launch-day performance immensely. That said, getting noticed and reviewed by these sites can be incredibly difficult. Because of their size and prominence, the most popular sites are inundated with requests like yours all the time. I recommend reaching out, after all there's no harm in trying, but don't be disappointed if you don't hear back. Often times, these sites are just too busy to take on yet another review.

That said, there are other ways to garner promotion and press. You may just have to think a bit differently. Consider promoting your software through smaller or more local channels. If your software is targeted at the general public, you may consider contacting a local news outlet, niche blog, or community newsletter group. These outlets, while significantly less popular than big review sites, still have potentially tens of thousands of readers and a vested interest in promoting the community and the people that live there. They also receive requests like yours far less frequently. Often times, local community outlets will spotlight local artists and businesses. Keep in mind, these outlets are more vested in people than in their company, so you'll need to tailor submissions to fit that need. Instead of discussing the product, tell the story of your business: Describe your business briefly. What do you do? Why did you set out to start a business? Do you work nights and weekends or did you quit your job? Has the community helped you in any way? How long have you been working on your software and how does it feel to finally launch? These are the questions that community outlets find interesting. Once you have a couple hundred words describing your story, send it in and ask if they'd consider publishing it. Most local news sites have an email address you can send inquiries to. If they enjoy your story, you may even get the chance to sit down for an interview with a journalist or write a short column describing yourself, your business, and the problems your products solve. It may seem like advice from the old world of media, but an old-world audience is still an audience.

PRESS RELEASES AND SOCIAL MEDIA

Before you launch, you'll need to craft your launch-day press releases. Ideally, you should draft a blog post and newsletter email first. These two mediums are your bread and butter, and since they're the two mediums most under your control, you have a lot of flexibility when it comes to the presentation and format. Your announcement posts, which essentially function as press releases, should focus on the narrative you want surrounding your release. Your post should discuss the product, what it does, what problems it solves, and where it's going next. You should also consider discussing the motivations behind a given announcement. Why did you choose the features you did? Why is this product or service useful? Why did you decide to build it? Why now? Your answers to these questions guide the reader towards a better understanding of the value you are providing. They offer a convincing case for your software, and drive the user to consider the possibility that they may actually be unsatisfied with their current set of solutions to the same problem. Better yet, you may be able to demonstrate to the reader that there is a problem that they are unaware of, and your software can help make their life better or easier.

It's important to note that this discussion isn't just useful for launch-day posts. The process described here works for any and all product announcements you make whether the announcement is for new features or a new product entirely.

	Reddit	Hacker News
Adventurer's Codex Launch Day Announcement	200+ upvotes 3,200 page-views	N/A
d20.photos Launch Day Announcment	230+ upvotes 3,000+ page-views	N/A
Python 3.5 and Multitasking Blog Post	N/A	4,000 page-views #5 on the front page
YouTube RSS Feeds Blog Post	N/A	16,000 page-views #2 on the front page

Once you have a blog post or newsletter email drafted, it's time to use that material to draft a custom announcement post for each platform you're going to use to promote your product. Remember, each community on the Web is different. The platforms incentivize different things and users on those platforms are looking for different types of content. Twitter, for example, incentivizes simple messages or stories that can easily be chunked into individual posts in a longer thread. These conversations might cause a user to click on a story, but not always. Users browsing Twitter tend to stay on Twitter, rather than follow links to external sites. Tweets, therefore, should summarize the story succinctly, and give users the most information possible to encourage them to seek more. This rule is largely true for Facebook as well. Users there are more likely to read the article summary, or click through to a Facebook Page or Group, rather than leave the site. Reddit and Hacker News, on the other hand, are essentially content aggregators. Users there expect to be taken to other sites. On Reddit and Hacker News, post titles should be short, catchy, and encourage the users to find out more by clicking the link and reading the full post. Customizing your release for each platform is important. Once you leave the safe harbors of your own site and newsletter, you're largely at the whims of fickle algorithms, and appeasing them is required for success. Some algorithms, like those that power Hacker News and Reddit, are fairly well understood and straightforward to please. Others, like those used by Facebook, YouTube, and Twitter, are more convoluted and the algorithms themselves are black-boxed. Pleasing them is difficult and based largely on heuristics and hearsay, but that doesn't mean you shouldn't try.

Personally, I've had mixed results promoting my software on social media. While I have been lucky enough to see a few of my blog posts reach the front page of Hacker News (and Adventurer's Codex announcements continuously do well on Reddit), the ecosystems of Twitter and Facebook have been a lot harder to appease. Below is a breakdown of how well my various software releases and blog posts have done on both Reddit and Hacker News on the day they came out. I've excluded Facebook and Twitter results from this table because both platforms attracted so little traffic as to be completely negligible.

As you can see from these results, Reddit and Hacker News can drive substantial traffic to your site. That said, tailoring your post to a specific community and platform can be challenging. Communities on Reddit especially have strict rules regarding promoting paid services or the user's own content. These rules can make it hard to promote your software depending on the community you're targeting. Hacker News is far more amenable to product announcements, but I've found that it's harder to gain traction there because all content competes for the same space on the front page. On Reddit, each community can set its own priorities and promote its own interests separate from the Reddit user base as a whole.

You may notice that the two blog posts listed in the table above both made it to the front page of Hacker News, and they were both listed in the top ten posts on the site that day. Given that, you should note the fairly large difference in page-views between them. My blog post that reached #2 on Hacker News had four times the traffic of my post just three slots away. In my experience, traffic on Hacker News decays exponentially. That is, the #2 post gets a small fraction of the number of page-views relative to the #1 post. The #3 post gets a smaller fraction relative to the #2, and so forth. On Reddit this trend doesn't really appear to hold for niche communities. I've found that posts on Reddit gain significant popularity if they're on the first page, but page-view counts don't seem to vary as much based on the order of the posts on any given page. Hacker News is not so forgiving.

So far, we've focused on crafting blog posts and posting content to social media sites for our launch day announcements, but there are two other platforms that can be incredibly useful to you when you're lining up your initial release.

Product Hunt is a site that helps users find and share interesting new products and services on the Web. Its staff review and promote sites based on their novelty, usefulness, and other factors. The site is free and requires no setup for users looking to browse and recommend sites, but creators or product owners need to jump through a few hoops before they're allowed to post their products. This process can take up to a week before you're able to finally post your products, so get started on this process early on. Being on Product Hunt, while not a guarantee of success, is a great step towards getting your site in front of a larger audience, plus there's the chance your product gets featured on the front page. Though rare, getting featured by Product Hunt's editorial team can really improve your launch-day performance. Pine.blog saw more traffic in one day after being featured by Product Hunt than it had in weeks before-hand (Pine.blog was submitted to, and promoted on, Product Hunt months after launch). However, even if you're not featured, Product Hunt provides an outlet that can help announce your product to the world. Product Hunt, like Hacker News, is a source for many other algorithmically-driven promotional sites, and being featured on either site tends to drive traffic from other parts of the Web.

Indie Hackers is another community that can serve you well when you decide to launch. The site is tailored towards creators and developers who build stuff on the Web independently (as the name suggests). The site resembles Hacker News, but it offers significantly more community features. Indie Hackers allows creators to profile their journey and submit milestones. While I haven't used the site much, various releases of Pine.blog have attracted both constructive and complimentary feedback, which I've appreciated a lot. You may find that there is more to gain from Indie Hacker's community boards and advice sections, but at the bare minimum the site functions as yet another distribution channel for your product announcements.

While each of these platforms and services provides methods to get the word out on launch day, they also serve a few additional purposes. First, by posting your releases on such a broad array of services, you're increasing the chances that one of them does work well. Going viral on the internet is partly a function of ones own work, but it's also partly luck. Secondly, a post on another platform helps legitimize your software in the eyes of search engines. This cross-posting is yet another SEO technique. Sites are more highly ranked if they're linked to from other credible sites. By cross-posting your releases on each of these platforms, and (importantly) linking back to your own site, you help improve your site's ranking. This is probably the single most significant impact of your promotions day-to-day, because the majority of people discover new sites and services via search engines. To this day, Adventurer's Codex receives nearly half of its users from Google search results. Promotional opportunities from sites like Hacker News, Product Hunt, Indie Hackers, Twitter, Reddit, and Facebook are good for getting the word out, but search engines keep spreading the word long after your posts fall off the front page and off the end of the time-line.

LAUNCH DAY

When launch day comes, it will likely be stressful. There's a lot to manage and track, which, in turn, generates a fair amount of anxiety. The night before your launch, make a checklist of the things you need to do. Hopefully, you'll already have your blog posts written, your social media posts drafted, and your newsletter email ready to send. That way, on the actual launch day (when your brain may be overloaded and stressed) you only need to follow the steps on your checklist. This reduces the possibility of mistakes and of overlooking critical promotional outlets.

Conventional marketing wisdom dictates that you choose a Tuesday, Wednesday, or Thursday to launch your software. This maxim claims that most people are too busy on Mondays and too checked-out on Fridays to pay attention to your release, and your reach will be more limited. This same wisdom claims that releases are ideally announced at 10 am U.S. Pacific Time be-cause the vast majority of Americans are awake, at work (where analytics confirm they probably aren't actually working a large part of the time), and finished with major morning commitments. People on the West Coast are done with meetings and people on the East Coast are just back from lunch. This time-slot doesn't balance the U.S. and European markets well though, so an East Coast time might be better if you are hoping to reach both markets. Personally, I believe the 10 am time-slot maxim is born out of a few key observations: Silicon Valley is on the West Coast so 10 am Pacific Time makes more sense for them, and large press gatherings tend to be scheduled around that time. In my experience, launching during said time-slot hasn't affected my releases in any notable way. I've launched software at night, during the morning, and in the afternoon; the specific time seems to have a negligible effect. However, there's something to be said for leveraging wisdom (or in this case, superstition) when it doesn't hurt. There are certain scenarios where adhering to such a strict maxim to launch only on Wednesdays at 10 am PT will result in significant issues. I've found that Wednesdays are particularly hard to schedule around because large companies like Apple, Google, and others tend to follow this precept as well. This means that it's possible you'll be releasing software at the same time as a major tech announcement, which only hurts your chances of getting attention. You simply can't compete with the tech giants. If you do plan on launching on a Wednesday, make sure that the major tech players haven't scheduled anything on that day.

Once you press the launch button, you'll most likely be tempted to sit around, watch your analytics, scour social media, and respond to feedback. This impulse is simultaneously valuable and destructive. After you launch, set aside an hour to manage your response. Use that time to watch your feeds, respond to comments, etc. After that hour, go for a walk or do something else to distract you for a bit. On a normal day, I'm able to use my work to distract me from other things, but on a launch day being by my computer or phone at all just results in me wasting time pouring through social media for people discovering my software. On launch days, I spend my time going for numerous walks, and my apartment ends up looking pretty clean by the end of it. My recommendation would be to alternate between your distraction activities as needed. Sitting by your computer or over your phone doesn't make the views or the likes come in faster; a watched pot and all that. Once you're sure that nothing is fundamentally broken, split your time between managing your release and doing literally anything else. This will help you manage your own expectations. If your launch goes well (even with thousands of comments or sign-ups), I've found that watching each one tick by is nerve-racking. It never feels successful enough at any given moment. That said, coming back after a long walk to a few hundred new users and comments feels fantastic, even if the total response for launch day is smaller.

Launch day and especially the day after, are more about your own expectations and reactions than they are about the software you actually released. Launch days are stressful precisely because they feel like a make or break moment; the end-all, be-all for your business. The final judgement. Everything you've been working towards, everything you've accomplished, is now in the court of public opinion to be scrutinized and critiqued, until your venture is deemed either a glorious triumph or a pathetic blunder. Launch day is the quintessential apex. A bad launch means you're a failure, and a good launch means you're a success, right?

The Aftermath & Beyond

If your launch was successful, that's fantastic! If it wasn't, don't worry too much about it. Unlike the rather provocative end to the previous section would have you believe, your launch day isn't nearly as relevant as most people think. Sure, it's great to actually launch software, and a good launch is a good opportunity to get some initial attention, but it's by no means a deciding factor when it comes to determining your software's success. A good launch is a kickstart, not a finish line. It helps set you up for success, but does not guarantee it (nor is it even strictly necessary). In my experience, software that doesn't get a strong boost at launch can be harder to boost later on, but that later boost is still quite achievable. Your launch, in no way, determines your outcome.

I've had a few really great, and also a few really disappointing launches, but the launch and subsequent growth of Adventurer's Codex is probably my most illustrative experience, so let's dive into that one specifically. Although the site was available and usable for months beforehand, we officially launched in September of 2016 with posts on Reddit, Facebook, and Twitter. These posts were the first public announcements we made about the software and, as I mentioned before, the Reddit posts did surprisingly well. Measuring page-views is hard and dependent on how you measure, but this graph from our Google Analytics at the time gives you a good general feel for how Adventurer's Codex has evolved.

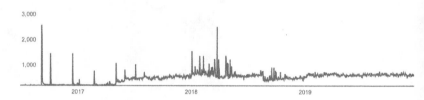

Keep in mind, with any Javascript-based analytics, especially Google Analytics, ad-blockers and modern tracker blockers will cause user counts to be lower than they actually are. In some sectors, especially those with tech-savvy users, ad-blockers result in 30% of your page-views going uncounted. This partly explains why the values seen in this chart don't necessarily match those found in the data from the prior section. That data is an aggregation, taking multiple sources into account.

As you can see from the graph, the launch day was rather successful, but after a week the traffic had gone back to essentially zero. The next few spikes are from additional feature releases and other promotions (we did a book giveaway early on, which was a lot of fun and garnered attention). It wasn't until around May of 2017, nearly nine months later that traffic reliably started to grow, and although we've never seen a single day's traffic reach the heights of our launch day, we get just as much traffic now every four days. As hard as it may be to believe, this pattern is actually incredibly common. Some readers will remember the viral hit game Flappy Bird from early 2014. At its height, its developer, Dong Nguyen, earned $50,000 a day from ads and sales. But (in a fact that has gone largely ignored by players and app-developers alike) the original game was released to the iOS and Android app stores in May of 2013, nearly nine months before it became a success.[35] While the nine-month timing of both Flappy Bird and Adventurer's Codex is a coincidence, the takeaway is clear: it may take time before your software sees any measurable success, and while launch days are important they don't decide your software's fate.

At this point, you may be feeling one of two ways: either you're relieved that your launch isn't the end-all you once thought, or you're even more disheartened because you thought that all the work necessary for your big payoff was done when actually it's just the beginning. In a rather convenient and utterly contrived way, this leads us back to the beginning of this book. Recall that our first ever discussion revolved around your single most important resource, the thing that keeps you going, keeps you trying new things, and pushes you onward: motivation. There's a reason we spent so much time discussing how to stay motivated, how to recharge, and how to think about, acquire, and spend this invaluable currency. In truth, you do not know how long it will take for your software to be commercially successful, if it ever is. You can only know your own limits and create your own timeline. Ultimately, what criteria you use to judge your software to be a commercial success is probably more important than the software you wrote to get there.

This is why designing powerful, feature-rich software that's easy and inexpensive to maintain is so valuable. If your software costs thousands of dollars to run each month, but doesn't gain a significant footing initially, you might very well cancel the project before that critical period ends. If you're working a full-time job and your software takes hours every week to maintain or improve, then this leads to a similar problem. Eventually, it won't be worth working on any longer; you'll lose interest, you'll stop fixing bugs, and the project will die. On the other hand, if your software and your business function on their own, then a small subsidy from you and a few hours a month can keep a product up and active forever.

LIVING ON THE LONG TAIL

Even if your software does really well at launch, as it ages and matures it will probably see a steady decline in revenue. The question then becomes: how long can the software sustain itself, and how long can you justify working on it?

David Smith, the iOS developer and podcaster also known as "underscore David Smith", discusses this idea at length on his podcast, "Under the Radar" with Marco Arment.[36] In the episode, "Apps as Annuities" from 2017, Smith discusses the way he thinks about independent software development and his own apps. He introduces the idea that his apps aren't single-ventures, they are instead one part of a diverse app portfolio. In his view, there are very few developers who hit upon one app (or service) that can support them financially for an extended period of time. Instead, he thinks of his software more like an investment, an annuity, that pays him back in gradual installments.

David Smith: [When I started] I was focused entirely on the development side of things. I was focused on the design side of things and the marketing, to some degree, but thinking of these broader business things wasn't something that was really on my radar at all and now, eight-and-a-half years later, it is something that I think about more and I realize the importance of thinking through... Depending on what you want your business to look like. How you want it to pay you and - both now and in the future - what your ultimate goals are. What impact the types of apps that make sense for you to build. Different apps have very different revenue curbs...

I took a look over the last eighteen months and I looked at what the revenue curve looked like for this app [Audiobooks], with no maintenance, no anything. It had just been sitting in the app store and the app makes its money from advertising and - to a very small degree - some app purchases for some kind of premium books. What was interesting to me was the curve that the revenue took, matched pretty closely to an exponential decay curve... the sales went down by half-a-percent per day...

> **David Smith (cont):** I release the app and then hopefully it pays me back over time and in many ways that's the same kind of thing that - in the financial world - we would call something like an annuity, which is where you take a large sum of money and you give it to a bank or an investment institution and they pay you an amount of money back each month...
>
> **Marco Arment:** I love the idea that you're living off of background noise. Like the asymptotic tails of all these curves and you just pile enough of them up and I have a background radiation income.
>
> #71 Apps as Annuities - Under the Radar Transcript, RelayFM

The asymptotic tails Arment is describing are the same tails we saw in our discussion of blogging. Sales of your service, after a certain point of growth, are logarithmic not linear. They don't just go to zero overnight, instead they decay. However, if you stack enough of them together through different apps and services, you can still generate a significant income between updates.

Interestingly, for a significant period in 2019, Adventurer's Codex traffic followed the opposite trend Smith describes. For several months, while the team was primarily focused on an internal refactor and we released no features at all, the site saw a steady 0.5% increase in traffic month-over-month.

Some developers and business owners find this business model unappealing because it forces them to build multiple apps and services instead of focusing on one flagship product. Now, I'm not suggesting that creating a flagship product or service is impossible nor do I mean to imply that your service can't grow after it launches. It's just that in my experience they're challenging to do right and relatively uncommon in the industry. Think about it — how big, how impactful, and how expensive does your idea need to be in order to single-handedly support you and your business? Conversely, how big, impactful, and expensive does your idea need to be if your goal is that it supplies just one quarter of that amount?

ONGOING PROMOTION

Hopefully by now you're convinced that marketing isn't just something you do before you launch or only on launch day. Marketing will be part of your job description for as long as your business exists, or at least it should be. Each time you release a new major version of your software, indeed every time you make any significant change, you should promote your efforts. Feature releases and updates follow a similar format to the one described in earlier chapters: write the announcement post and newsletter email, draft social media posts, coordinate a time and day for release, and then press the launch button. For significant features and releases you may even want to purchase ads or do some sort of promotion to garner interest.

Once you have an audience, consider doing giveaways. If your service is tied to some real commodity like books or music, then you have a ready source of material to give out. If your service is entirely virtual, consider getting stickers or patches made to promote your service and give those out at release-time. Marketing can be a creative endeavor and your efforts don't need to be purely virtual. Some software businesses advertise using billboards and while that will probably be out of your financial reach, you may want to try out more local forms of advertising like newspaper ads, posters, and flyers. Your goal is to promote your work and get people interested enough to try it out. Podcast appearances, guest blog posts, and interviews can be incredibly effective ways for you to tell your story and acquire users.

Using these methods, over time, you'll develop a regular pattern and a familiar flow that works for you and your business. Keep checklists of what works and doesn't and always aim to improve your efforts. An effective marketing strategy is challenging to construct and it takes time to mature and develop. Give yourself space to be creative, to experiment, and to fail, and don't be too hard on yourself when you do. Most of of the time your plans will fail to garner much attention, but that's ok. Move forward and find a better method.

PLANNING FOR THE FUTURE

Once you launch, you'll most likely be left with a significant number of features that didn't make the launch-day cut. These features have now become your feature roadmap., and they will guide you and your product design in the months and years to come. Write down everything you want your software to do, at all times. If product-designer you comes up with an idea and CEO you likes the idea, write it down. Keep a list of everything you'd like to build. Once you launch, work on prioritizing that list. You'll want to group features that are similar or that build towards a common goal or story; features that share a common purpose are easier to market. Set out to release something regularly, and prioritize regular updates over larger ones. Updating your software on a consistent, relatively frequent basis shows your customers that you're still working on and improving the software, and regular updates serve a motivational purpose: releasing your work can help push you forward and keep you excited. Big releases, while often immensely satisfying when they finally launch, often take a significant period of time to develop and market. Infrequent, large releases are great if you can stay afloat and motivated until they're completed, but especially in the early phases such a strategy can be dangerous.

Work on improving your processes. If your deployment process takes down your site for a few minutes, work on a simple zero-downtime solution. This can be as simple as running two instances of your application at once and upgrading one at a time (something Marco Arment recommends in his guide that we discussed in Part 2). Prioritize features and bugs according to their impact on your users. If something is easy to improve or fix and important to your users, then that change should be given priority over other features or bugs that take longer to build or are less impactful.

Release Checklists

Before you begin working on a new release, put together a feature checklist of everything you're intending to ship in the given version. You can organize this list in whatever way is most useful to you, but I prefer to break features down into the following categories:

- **Headlining Features:** Features that will be in the marketing material and sold as the major new features of this version.

- **Minor Features and Bug Fixes:** Other things that you want to make it into this release, but that aren't really worth promoting.

- **Gold Plating:** Features that would be nice to have, but that aren't required to ship.

These categories can help you keep track of your immediate accomplishments and give you some ability to gauge your progress version to version. Checking off these items serves a motivational purpose too. Finishing things feels good. If you don't track what you're doing, you can't get the satisfaction of checking it off the list when it's done.

Some developers will want to skip these recommendations entirely for a more scrum or Agile approach. While I've found that many aspects of the Agile process, particularly the retrospectives, can be really beneficial, following it completely imposes more process than is required for one person (or even a very small team).

Be aware of how much time you're dedicating to writing checklists or logging tickets. It's important to write things down so they aren't forgotten, and so that you have enough information to fix issues later. However, strict processes can slow you down and cause you to spend more time tracking the project than actually building it. Take a look at this Pine.blog feature checklist. Notice how the headlining features are at the top and the minor features are in a list below. Everyone will have their own method of tracking progress and I've found that handwritten feature lists work well for me. The exact format has evolved over time, but the structure is similar. As you can see, I also tend to sketch my UI in pencil before attempting to build anything.

A sample Pine.blog release checklist.

You may notice that one headline feature and one minor feature didn't get checked off; they have arrows next to them. These are features that were pushed off and deemed non-essential. Learning when to cancel or delay features is an important skill to develop.

CONSISTENCY

Above all, probably the single most important factor in determining the success of your business is your own consistency. How often you work and for how long matters a lot. Most software startups, and most businesses, fail. And most fail before they launch. That isn't to say that your business will succeed if it does launch, it may not. However, launching a product, like writing a book, is something many people dream of but significantly fewer achieve. Launching software is hard. Launching successful software is harder. But every day that you sit down to work through another bug, build another screen, write another test, or draft another blog post you're closer to launch than you were before you started.

Consistency is a hard thing to achieve and your success depends heavily on the world you live in. Life-events and world-events will impact your ability to set aside time to work and even when you do set aside time, those same events will impact your mental fortitude. Burnout will be a huge risk to your projects, and learning about, mitigating the possibility of, and recovering from burnout is an incredibly valuable skill for a business owner to have. Burnout comes in many forms, flavors, and sizes, and it impacts everyone it touches differently. Working long hours for little-to-no pay or fixing complicated and nuanced bugs late a night when you just want to go to bed can drive you mad and eventually burn you out. When this happens remember: it's ok. Take a break, heal, try again later. Like we discussed early on, the primary risk from burnout is to your own health and the secondary risk is to your willingness to continue. Most businesses fail because they don't launch. Burning the midnight oil and rushing to meet a deadline may work well occasionally, but risking your own mental health is a faustian bargain, and one you will not win. Launching software after a healthy, but extended development timeline is better than not launching at all. So often, we ignore crucial variables in our decision making. Your health, your fortitude, and your motivation is finite. You might think that you can work just a little harder, pull just a few more all-nighters, miss just few more nights out with friends, but your business doesn't exist in a vacuum. Every time you turn down an opportunity to recharge, you burn the wick down just a bit further. Sometimes this is completely fine, but other times you do more harm to yourself than you do good for the business.

WHAT ARE YOU WAITING FOR?

If, by some miracle, you've gotten through all of this and you're still looking to start a business and become independent, then you absolutely should. Contrary to how it may seem, my goal is not to dissuade you, only to provide context and to give you a fuller picture of just how large and how small an undertaking starting a business can be. Building a business and releasing software independently has been one of the great joys of my life. In building and releasing my own software, I've contributed to a number of great communities, met a huge number of fantastic people, and learned more than I ever thought I could about business and software development. Being an independent developer has, in short, made me a better person. It can do the same for you as well.

I write these words during a global pandemic and an extremely turbulent time in society, in politics, and in the lives of everyone I meet. Yet somehow, I've built and launched software in the midst of this crisis (Nine9s and d20.photos) and I wrote this book. In part this productivity has been because of the crisis not in spite of it. In dark or stressful times, it can be useful to carve out for yourself a space to be productive, to make a difference, to exert some modicum of control over your own life. In these times, writing software and writing this book have been that for me. Ascribing silver linings to terrible events often just cheapens the severity of the crisis. There is no silver lining to be found with a pandemic. Instead, I think of such events not as dark clouds with faint silver linings, but as punctuation marks. They force us to stop, they break the tedium of daily life and cause us to look around, to look back, and to look forward at what we are, what we have been, and what we could be. On the other side of this disaster, like with so many others, there will be a rebuilding. In the same way that society will rebuild, so will each of us. Perhaps then, this moment can provide the spark, the ignition to a fire that has been building in you for a long time.

In all aspects we see, with this moment of reflection, what needs to be done and what could be. While many in the world need a crisis to reflect and to invent, it is the job of the independent developer, of the entrepreneur, of the creator to always dream of what could be, and it is the job of those who can change the world to do so. As developers, we have the ability to shape conversations, to bridge divides, and to promote a better world by building software that furthers those goals. Your ideas, your software, and your business can change the world. Few other professions in history have the opportunities that we do. Software on the Web is relatively inexpensive to run and requires little work to maintain, yet it can reach a truly global audience.

Even though the world is full of huge companies and thousands of individuals trying to change the world, the scale of the

Web is truly enormous and there is always more to do and more people to do it with. No matter how big the Web gets, it will never be full. That is the promise of the Web and the opportunity that you, as an independent developer, can harness. Give it a shot, learn all you can, and launch something.

Acknowledgments

I have been incredibly lucky to have the love and support of my family and a network of long-time, trusted friends to help me through this process. My sincerest thanks to everyone who helped proofread, edit, and refine this book. Your work made all of this possible. Conversations with each of you helped shape the structure of this work and the contents within it. Your help in editing made this book what it has become. Your support has kept me going and driven me to complete a task that I once believed was beyond me. In these trying times, you've stood by and emboldened me.

Over the years I have been fortunate enough to meet an incredible array of smart people. From the floors of tech conferences to the cramped rooms of meetup spaces, from the halls of academia to the break rooms at the places I've worked, from the tables at our favorite coffeeshops to the counters at the most unassuming bars, your conversations and your passion for the work you do pushes me to think harder, to dive deeper, and to be better than I ever could alone. You tolerated, and even encouraged, my discussions of technology, tech culture, and societal change. You gave me chances to branch out to try new things and to take on new challenges. You trusted me to solve problems and you encouraged me when I needed it. In truth, while this book was written following the launch of Nine9s in June of 2020, my journey towards this point began long ago: at a local programming meetup, with an open-mic night, and with the founding of Adventurer's Codex with Jim and Nathaniel. It continued through Codebiosys with Marco, Jason, and Dave and onto the current day. Over the years I've been lucky enough to work on great software with even better people, I've made friends, and they've made me a better person. This book is as much from them as from me.

A special thanks goes to my editor Jenn. She didn't have to take on the insane prospect of wrangling my thoughts and words, deciphering their jumbled meaning, and forcing them into coherence, but she did. Without her help, this book would have been nothing more than a jumbled series of informal blog posts strung together with a bit of chicken-wire and run-on sentences.

Thank you.

Notes and References

[1] Sole proprietorship. Wikipedia.
https://en.wikipedia.org/wiki/Sole_proprietorship

[2] Partnership. Wikipedia.
https://en.wikipedia.org/wiki/Partnership

[3] Corporation. Wikipedia.
https://en.wikipedia.org/wiki/Corporation

[4] Limited liability company. Wikipedia.
https://en.wikipedia.org/wiki/Limited_liability_company

[5] An App Store Experiment. AppStories.
https://stories.appbot.co/how-i-got-2-3m-app-downloads-without-spend-ing-a-cent-on-marketing-f4823b6bc779

[6] Scanning the Commons? Evidence on the Benefits to Startups Participating in Open Standards Development. DM Waguespack, L Fleming. Management Science, 2009.
https://pubsonline.informs.org

[7] Flyway. Redgate.
https://flywaydb.org

[8] Django Release Schedule
https://www.djangoproject.com/download/

[9] A drafting metaphor would probably be more apt, especially since fish aren't known to wear coats with tails as far as I know.

[10] Securing Your Server. Linode.
https://www.linode.com/docs/security/securing-your-server/

[11] System design for Twitter. Twitter.
https://medium.com/@narengowda/system-design-for-twitter-e737284afc95

12 How To Use Celery with RabbitMQ to Queue Tasks on an Ubuntu VPS. Digital Ocean.
https://www.digitalocean.com/community/tutorials/how-to-use-celery-with-rabbitmq-to-queue-tasks-on-an-ubuntu-vps

[13] pg_dump. Postgres Documentation.
https://www.postgresql.org/docs/9.1/app-pgdump.html

[14] Chapter 23. Backup and Restore. Postgres Documentation.
https://www.postgresql.org/docs/8.1/backup.html

[15] Automatically test your database backups. Marco Arment.
https://marco.org/2017/02/01/db-backup-testing

[16] Redash helps you make sense of your data. Redash
https://redash.io

[17] Simple Notifications. Pushover.
https://pushover.net

[18] How to Secure Your Server. Linode.
https://www.linode.com/docs/security/securing-your-server/

[19] Security in Django. Django Documentation.
https://docs.djangoproject.com/en/3.1/topics/security/

[20] Security. Postgres Documentation.
https://www.postgresql.org/docs/7.0/security.htm

[21] Git Pre-Commit Hook Script. Sonictherocketman GitHub Gist
https://gist.github.com/Sonictherocketman/
b196995f768eda4411e0771e9c509237

[22] Foxconn suicides. Wikipedia.
https://en.wikipedia.org/wiki/Foxconn_suicides

[23] Child labour in the fashion supply chain. The Guardian.
https://labs.theguardian.com/unicef-child-labour/

[24] Green Data Centers. Equinix.
https://www.equinix.co.uk/data-centers/design/green-data-centers/

[25] Climate Impact Disclosure. Nine9s.
https://nine9s.cloud/kb/infrastructure

[26] Web Hosting For App Developers. Marco Arment
https://marco.org/2014/03/27/web-hosting-for-app-developers

[27] How To Set Up Django with Postgres, Nginx, and Gunicorn on Ubuntu 18.04. Digital Ocean.
https://www.digitalocean.com/community/tutorials/how-to-set-up-django-with-postgres-nginx-and-gunicorn-on-ubuntu-18-04

[28] Sample Docker Configuration. Sonictherocketman. GitHub Gist.
https://gist.github.com/Sonictherocketman/989415b74713cc06259b2d-b861aa32f2

[29] Sample CentOS Setup Scripts. Sonictherocketman.
https://gist.github.com/Sonictherocketman/bf6bb6264e870ae8981093e-f777db105

[30] How to Encrypt Your Data with dm-crypt. Linode.
https://www.linode.com/docs/security/encryption/encrypt-data-disk-with-dm-crypt/

[31] proxy_pass isn't working when SELinux is enabled, why?. Stack Overflow.
https://stackoverflow.com/questions/27435655/proxy-pass-isnt-working-when-selinux-is-enabled-why#28834275

[32] YouTube vs Grey: A Ballad of Accidental Suspension. CGP Grey. YouTube. https://www.youtube.com/watch?v=DIssymQvrbU

[33] Short-form Blogging. Gina Trapani
http://scribbling.net/2014/10/16/short-form-blogging/

[34] A Brief Discussion On Screen Etiquette. Adventurer's Codex.
https://adventurerscodex.com/update/2017/01/04/screen-gaming.html

[35] Flappy Bird. Wikipedia.
https://en.wikipedia.org/wiki/Flappy_Bird

[36] #71: Apps as Annuities. Under the Radar (RelayFM)
https://www.relay.fm/radar/71